CREATIVE EXCUSES

EVERY OCCASION

CREATIVE EXCUSES

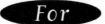 *For*

EVERY OCCASION

*Old Standards, Innovative Evasions, and
Blaming the Dog*

ANDREW FROTHINGHAM
and **TRIPP EVANS**

St. Martin's Press ₥ *New York*

To Clyde Taylor—
the book was *his* idea.

CREATIVE EXCUSES FOR EVERY OCCASION. Copyright ©
1995 by Andrew Frothingham and Tripp Evans. All rights
reserved. Printed in the United States of America. No part of this
book may be used or reproduced in any manner whatsoever without written permission except in the case of brief quotations
embodied in critical articles or reviews. For information, address
St. Martin's Press, 175 Fifth Avenue, New York, N.Y. 10010.

Design by Junie Lee

Library of Congress Cataloging-in-Publication Data

Evans, Tripp.
    Creative excuses for every occasion : old standards, innova-
tive evasions, and blaming the dog / Andrew Frothingham and
Tripp Evans.
        p.   cm.
    "A Thomas Dunne book."
    ISBN 0-312-13042-2
    1. Excuses—Humor.   I. Frothingham, Andrew.   II. Title.
PN6231.E87E89   1995
818'.5402—dc20   95-1776
                                                         CIP
A Thomas Dunne Book

First Edition: June 1995

10 9 8 7 6 5 4 3 2 1

contents

introduction

Excuses separate us from other animals; they are an essential part of our civilization. Explaining away actions or inactions with a good excuse demonstrates a sophisticated mental process and prevents hurt feelings and further conflicts. What's more, excuses are often the best way to protect your reputation and cover your ass.

One would think that such a vital aspect of our society would have reached higher levels of finesse. But no. Most people rely on the same old excuses over and over. There's no longer any excuse for this. Read *Creative Excuses for Every Occasion* for inspiration and you'll never have to rely on your "dead grandmother" again.

format

We have divided the excuses for each topic into three types:

The Old Standards
Each section starts with three or more excuses we've all heard before. They're so common, if you use one, you'd better be prepared to have it checked out. If one of "the old standards" happens to be true, use it. If this excuse is checked out, your reputation for unquestionable integrity will be upheld.

The More Creative
Here we present five or more excuses that are fun and creative.

We've found that the more imaginative and preposterous the excuse, the more likely people will assume it must be true. For example, "The reason I'm late is because my car was stolen, used in a robbery, and then impounded as evidence, so I had to take the bus" is more likely to be believed than, "My car wouldn't start until noon."

The Dog

We've included one dog excuse in each section in recognition of the beloved, ultimate excuse, "The dog ate my homework."

one

Societal

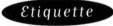
Etiquette

Being unable to attend an event

The Old Standards
- I'd love to come but the in-laws are in from out-of-town.
- I have a cold and it might be contagious.
- I wish you had mentioned it sooner. Unfortunately, I'm busy that night.
- We can't find a babysitter.

The More Creative
- I'm on maneuvers then. If I tell you any more, security regulations require that I kill you.
- I never go out when Mercury is retrograde.
- I'd love to come, as long as you're cool with the fact that I'm a smoker. I really can't live without a couple of cigars an hour.
- No can do. The moon is full that night, and I have to stay home for everyone's protection. Please don't ask me to explain.

- I have to finish writing a major presentation for a business meeting scheduled for 8 A.M. tomorrow. This is what I get for waiting until the last minute.

The Dog
- We just adopted a puppy and he howls whenever we leave him alone.

Not attending an event you had accepted

The Old Standards
- I wrote down the wrong date.
- I took a nap, and slept right though it.
- My car broke down and I couldn't make it.

The More Creative
- I had it all written down on my appointment book at work, but then I got fired. They escorted me out of the building and they won't send me the contents of my desk until after the investigation.
- It's your fault—you were supposed to remind me.
- I spent some time unexpectedly in jail.
- You mean the party was this year?
- It was one of those "stay-home-for-once-or-get-a-divorce" things.
- I thought it was canceled.
- I had a relapse.

The Dog
- I was planning to come, but the dog ate my wedding ring which was next to some table scraps by the sink. I had to follow the damned mutt all night so I'd be sure to be there when the ring reappeared, if you know what I mean.

Being late

The Old Standards

- My watch stopped.
- I overslept.
- The traffic was horrible.
- I got lost.

The More Creative

- I'm late, I'm taking Prozac, who cares?
- I was having an out-of-body experience.
- I got tied-up at the office. Bondage is so time-consuming.
- I forgot to reset my watch when I got in from Monaco.
- I wanted to give you extra time to get ready. I know how you hate to be rushed.
- I'm dyslexic and I switched the numbers of the address. I ended up at a massage parlor somewhere in the Bronx.
- The cab driver didn't speak English, so first he drove us to his house in Harlem so his eight-year-old could translate.
- My car was stolen and used in a robbery, and then it was impounded as evidence, so I had to take the bus.
- I have problems with meetings at this time—it's the hour my mother died.
- My "inner child" was dawdling.
- Actually, in many cultures being late is a sign of great respect.
- I think our culture is too time-oriented, don't you?

The Dog

- My dog got so excited he jumped up at the car window and accidentally pushed down the door lock. It took us two hours to get him out.

Bringing uninvited guests

The Old Standards
- They showed up at the last minute. I hope you don't mind that I brought them along.
- I tried to call, but your line was busy.
- We were sure you would have invited them if you had known they were in town.

The More Creative
- I thought you knew. We don't go anywhere without our bodyguards.
- We've decided that it's time to widen our cozy little circle of friends, and we thought these lovely people would be perfect additions.
- We had to bring them. They're seriously depressed and we're watching them to be sure they don't kill themselves.
- They're writing a book about us and they go everywhere with us.
- We're both on diets, but we know how much effort you put into your cooking. So we brought along a pair of designated eaters.
- They're cousins from the old country and they asked us to introduce them to a perfect American family; you were the ideal choice.
- We brought them along as a favor to you. They're location scouts. If they choose your house as a set for a commercial or a movie, you'll get paid thousands of dollars!

The Dog
- We had planned to leave them at our place, but the dog wouldn't stop humping their legs.

Bringing uninvited kids

The Old Standards
- Our sitter canceled at the last minute.
- Our kids are so well behaved that we figured you wouldn't mind.
- We know how much you love the little darlings.

The More Creative
- Ever since that incident with the priest, they freak out when left alone with strangers.
- We're hoping that if we don't exclude them now, they won't exclude us when we are old and senile.
- If we don't watch them every minute, they might run away.
- We had to bring them—it's the only way to safeguard against kidnapping.
- What?! Leave them somewhere where aliens could duplicate them and put robots in their place?
- Shhh—those aren't kids . . . they're very sensitive midgets.
- It's one of the terms of their probation that we not leave them with unsuspecting strangers.
- We didn't want to bring them, but it was the only way they'd let us have the car.

The Dog
- If we're not around, Sparky attacks the kids. One more bite and the judge says the poor dog gets put to sleep.

Being overdressed

The Old Standards
- I guess I'm a bit old-fashioned.
- I came right from the office and didn't have time to change.

- That part of the invitation was smudged. I thought it said something about your address, and I already know where you live.

The More Creative

- My outplacement counselor says to be prepared for an interview at all times.
- I'm writing a novel about Victorian England and it helps me write in the proper tone if I'm just a bit formal in my attire.
- I haven't had a chance to wear this stuff in years and I thought I'd get it out just for a lark.
- I look so young that people don't take me seriously unless I have a power suit on.
- I know I'm a bit overdressed—but I have to go from here to The White House.
- You never know when you might be abducted by aliens, and I want people from other planets to have a good impression of humans.
- I've decided to revive the aristocracy, and the first step is to start dressing better.
- You think this is overdressed? You should see what I look like when I really want to make an impression.

The Dog

- I had to come dressed up. The dog got territorial and marked all my casual clothes.

Being underdressed

The Old Standards

- I had to come right from work.
- I haven't had time to do the laundry.
- I thought this was a casual affair.

The More Creative
- I want to be sure you love me for who I am, not for my clothes.
- I gave up fashion for Lent.
- I read somewhere that dressing well greatly increases your chances of being kidnapped.
- My public relations consultant wants me to develop the common touch.
- I broke up with my girlfriend/boyfriend recently. Unfortunately, she/he didn't take it very well and snuck into my place when I wasn't there and cut the sleeves off of all my clothes.
- I was robbed. The thief made off with all my good clothes.

The Dog
- The children dressed the dogs up for a dog wedding, and my best clothes are covered with hair.

Not eating food prepared by the host

The Old Standards
- I'm a vegetarian.
- I had no idea it was a dinner party. I ate just before I got here.
- Sorry, I'm allergic to (fill in food).

The More Creative
- I think I saw something moving in the lobster bisque.
- I'm on a special diet and I can only eat foods with the letters *l*, *t* **and** *f* in them. So far the only food I've been able to find is a Thai dish made with lemon grass, tomatoes, and a strange fish that starts with an *f*. Or is it a *ph*?
- I can't believe it! We had beef Wellington mole and sesame noodles with a glazed brown sugar mustard sauce last night.
- I'm sorry, I can't eat this. This is the exact meal my mother chose the night before she was executed. She was innocent, by the way.

- I can't eat this meatloaf. Haven't you heard? There is a rumor that cows have been added to the endangered species list.

The Dog
- This is my dog's favorite meal. I wouldn't think of eating it. Could I have a doggie bag?

Relationships

Not talking about your feelings

The Old Standards
- I don't want to.
- I'll just get hurt.
- You wouldn't understand.

The More Creative
- I experience my emotions on a pre-verbal level. To refine them through language is to change and corrupt them.
- I take seriously the Miranda warning: anything I say can and will be used against me.
- Every time I talk about my feelings, I get a migraine headache.
- Who do you think you are, my shrink?
- I was brought up in a culture where speaking about emotions was a sign of weakness.
- You humans are so irrational. We Vulcans have no word that corresponds to your "feelings."
- To me, "feelings" is just the title of a sappy song. I believe in action.
- I think I've proven myself through what I've done. What could words possibly add?
- I'm a lawyer. I'm trained to argue, not to reveal.
- All this feelings stuff is so manipulative. You try and make the other person do what you want so your feelings won't be hurt. It's like dealing with my mother all over again. Forget it.

The Dog
- You want to know what makes for a successful relationship? Not talking. If people could get along with each other as well as I get along with my dog, there'd be fewer wars.

Declining or breaking a date

The Old Standards
- It wouldn't be a good idea, I'm not over my last relationship.
- I think I'm coming down with something.
- A client has unexpectedly come into town and I have to entertain him.
- Not tonight. I have to stay home and wash my hair.

The More Creative
- I'd have to get permission from my psychiatrist first.
- I can't. I'm still on probation after what happened to my last date.
- I don't date. I promised my mother I wouldn't date without getting her permission first and she died when I was 11.
- There. You've gone and ruined it by asking. That's so unromantic. Why couldn't we have just known deeply what the other one was thinking. Words are so crude.
- No, I couldn't. You're the type I always get into trouble with.
- It would be astrologically disastrous. You were born on a planet with only one moon.
- I'd miss the (fill in the name of your favorite 1960s or 70s sitcom) rerun.
- I just had my numbers done and it turns out to be a very bad day for me.

The Dog
- Every time I leave the dog alone, she takes revenge by uprooting all my rubber trees.

Taking Too Long to Get Ready

The Old Standards
- I lost sight of the time.
- I couldn't find anything to wear.
- Well, you want me to look nice, don't you?

The More Creative
- People expect me to be late, and I don't like to let them down.
- I was making a special outfit just for this occasion and the sewing machine broke so I had to sew it by hand.
- I got lost in a daydream. I was thinking about how lucky I am to have such a loving, understanding boyfriend/girlfriend and the time just got away from me.
- I was on the phone with the President. He's polling the country, and wanted to know what our feelings were regarding universal healthcare coverage.
- I was ready an hour ago, but while I was waiting I must have fallen asleep.

The Dog
- My dog had a minor stroke, and I had to resuscitate her by massaging her heart. She's twelve, it was going to happen sooner or later.

Not Getting Married

The Old Standards
- I'm too young.
- I'm too old.
- I have to concentrate on my career.
- I don't have the time.
- I haven't found the right person.
- I'm too set in my ways.
- We don't want kids, so why get married?

The More Creative
- The words "I do" sound too much like "doo-doo."
- I would get married, but I'm afraid of the blood test.
- I was looking for a girl like the one Dad married, but my mother turned me down.
- He's/She's been married three times already.
- I can't stand writing thank-you notes, and I know if I got married, people would send presents.
- Not getting married is the surest way of making sure you'll never get divorced.
- Filing joint returns is just too complicated.
- I can't get married until after my sister does. It's family tradition. And my sister's a nun.
- I'm married to my work. It was a lovely ceremony, really.
- Our signs aren't compatible; he's/she's an Aries and I'm a Leo.
- I'm married to my God.
- If we got married, I'm sure we'd start to take each other for granted.
- I promised my (<u>fill in name of relative</u>) before he/she died that I'd stay single.

The Dog
- Our dogs don't get along.

Breaking Up with Someone

The Old Standards
- I guess I'm just not ready to commit.
- I need some space.
- I'm not good enough for you.

The More Creative
- I've developed a skin condition and I have to avoid all excitement for a while so it will go away.

- I went through past-life regression and in Ancient Egypt we were brother and sister. So we can't be lovers—it would be like incest.
- You make me deliriously happy—but to succeed as an artist, I need to be miserable.
- You love me so unconditionally that I lose my drive to be more. You're bad for my business initiative.
- My parents really like you, but I have this thing—I can't be attracted to someone my parents like.
- I can't deal with someone being so nice to me; I'm not used to it—it's disorienting.
- Couples start to look alike, and I couldn't stand it if I started to look like you.
- I'm into the chase. Now that we've been together, there's no mystery.
- I like your fantasies so much I'm switching sexual orientations.
- Being with you has helped me see the light. I'm becoming a nun/monk.

The Dog
- I love you, but my dog doesn't like you.

Not Getting Divorced

The Old Standards
- We're staying together for the kids.
- We've been through too much together.
- The devil you know is better than the devil you don't know.
- My church doesn't recognize divorce.

The More Creative
- It would be more hassle than it is worth to try to divide all our assets.
- We're trying to work things out in couples therapy.

- Neither of us can afford a divorce right now.
- We both hate lawyers so much, we'd rather stay together and be miserable than give one penny to those bloodsuckers.
- We have a pre-nuptial agreement. If we divorce, I'll have to give up (fill in with name of an expensive item).
- We tried to get divorced, but our lawyers fell in love and ran away together.
- The last thing I want to hear is my parents telling me, "We told you so."
- No one in my family has ever been divorced. If I get a divorce, they'll disown me.
- If we got a divorce, we'd end up commuting to work separately, and we wouldn't be able to take advantage of the HOV (High Occupancy Vehicle) lane.
- Affairs are much more fun when you're married.
- I want a divorce, but I refuse to initiate one. The person who initiates the divorce usually loses.
- I'd have to learn how to program the CD player and the VCR.
- Being married is what makes me attractive to the opposite sex; they think I'm safe.

The Dog
- Neither one of us could bear living without Scruffy.

Being Divorced

The Old Standards
- He/She just didn't understand me.
- We were too young when we got married and we grew away from each other.
- My spouse couldn't cope with my success.
- I made the mistake of thinking I could help my spouse change, but it just doesn't work that way.
- We weren't right for each other.

The More Creative

- I discovered after we were married that most of his/her family had been institutionalized, and I was concerned that any children we had might inherit his/her insanity genes.
- Man wasn't created to live with just one person for a whole lifetime. It just isn't natural.
- My spouse had a crazy psychotherapist who was jealous of our relationship and wanted to break us apart.
- My spouse's family never liked me and they worked against me the whole time. Eventually, they won.
- My spouse couldn't cope with aging. I was a constant reminder of how old we really were, so I had to go.
- He/She isn't up for parole for another thirty years.
- My spouse joined a cult.
- It wasn't a real marriage. We just did it for immigration purposes.
- I realized I married my father/mother.

The Dog

- I said, "It's me or the dog." I lost.

Missing a Birthday

The Old Standards

- I was out of town and I didn't have your phone number.
- Believe it or not, I've been carrying around your card for a week. I kept forgetting to put it in the mail.
- I didn't think you wanted people to make a big thing of it anymore.

The More Creative

- I was staying at a place that didn't have a phone/fax machine/e-mail.
- Gosh—you never seem to age, so I never remember your birthday.

- Only negative people celebrate birthdays. If you don't pay attention to birthdays, you won't age.
- Life begins at conception. We'll celebrate tonight.
- I was waiting until Monday. I think you, like George Washington and Martin Luther King, should have your birthday celebrated by a long weekend.
- I think birthdays are for kids. Besides, you forgot mine. Nyahhh, Nyahhh.
- You are always saying you're a self-made man, and I didn't want to contradict you.
- To tell the truth, I hate birthdays. It was my mother's eightieth birthday and we used those candles that relit every time you tried to blow them out. She kept blowing them out and they kept relighting, but while we were all laughing, she suffered a cerebral hemorrhage and died.

The Dog
- I got confused about dog years and people years and I thought we humans only celebrated once every seven years.

Not Writing a Letter

The Old Standards
- I lost your address.
- I couldn't find a pen.
- I did write. Didn't you get it? That darned post office . . .
- My computer's down.

The More Creative
- I'm saving all my writing for my memoirs.
- Writing is so limiting. I need a more expressive medium.
- I guess I'm just one of those phone generation people.
- Writing is not a twentieth century form of communication; I'm into a more multimedia approach.
- I thought you were going to be out of town, so why send a

letter when you wouldn't be there? It would just sit in your mailbox.

- You and I are fluid; we live in the moment. It would be a sacrilege to put any of our interchange into a static medium like writing.
- My father is a lawyer. I've been trained never to put anything in writing.
- If I wrote you and that caused a crazed, gun-toting mail carrier to come to your door and kill you, I could never forgive myself!
- I'm conflicted. I only like scented stationery; but perfume is now politically incorrect.

The Dog
- I wrote you. But the puppy licked all my stamps together.

Not Answering the Phone

The Old Standards
- I didn't hear it ring.
- I knew it wouldn't be for me.
- I was in the shower.

The More Creative
- They've almost finished my replacement. All they need is a voice print to copy. But I'm smarter than those damn aliens!
- It was probably burglars calling to see if we're home. Now they think we aren't. So when they come over I'll finally get a chance to try out my new Uzi.
- I once answered the phone and got bad news. I'm smart enough to learn from stuff like that.
- No completed call, no income to the phone monopolies! Got to fight them somehow.
- I'm in training to be an executive. In upper management, we don't answer our own phones.

- You really want to know? I was "unavailable." You know what that means? I was in the bathroom. How far do you want me to go with the details?

The Dog
- I ran for the phone, but the dog thought it was a game and tackled me before I could get there.

Not Returning a Phone Call

The Old Standards
- I never got your message.
- I called you back, but your line was busy.
- I thought you said you'd call me again.
- I thought my husband/wife/roommate/secretary was going to return the call.
- By the time I got home it was late and I didn't want to wake you.

The More Creative
- I had to keep my phone line open. I was expecting a call from the terrorists who are holding my brother hostage.
- My phone is being tapped. I can't use it.
- Jesus—that was you? I couldn't recognize the voice because the tape in my machine is getting old, and I've been driving myself nuts trying to figure out who it was.
- I didn't think you really wanted me to call back. Your tone on the phone message was so mechanical that I thought you were the machine, and the machine was the person. It's not just what you say, it's how you say it.
- I tried to call you back, but the line was busy. Meanwhile your voice on the message got to me. That deep sexy voice got me all riled up. And I couldn't wait to see you. And then I fell asleep smoking and almost burned the house down.

The Dog
- The puppy chewed through the phone cord.

Ending a Phone Conversation

The Old Standards
- Oh, I just remembered, I left the stove on—I must run.
- My mom/dad/sister/brother/boss is on the other line. I've got to go.
- I can't keep talking, I have to keep the line open for an important call.
- I have to go put a quarter in the parking meter.

The More Creative
- I've got to go. Someone's trying to ring through on "call waiting."
- My spouse forbids me to discuss such matters.
- Don't say another word. I heard a click and I think we're being bugged. I'll call you when I've had the office swept and I know it's safe.
- Stop right now. You're getting into a topic that I'm writing about and I don't want it ever said that I stole ideas from you.
- I learned in time management classes that all important information can be conveyed within three minutes. Your time is up.
- Talking is unecological—it uses up too much oxygen. . . .
- Talking is so unevolved—let's try telepathy.

The Dog
- Must run, old bean; my old mutt is losing bladder control by the day and if I'm not home in a jiffy, Grandma's Oriental hall rug will be floating.

Leaving the Toilet Seat in the Wrong Position

The Old Standards
- I don't put it down at my house.
- It wouldn't stay up.
- Between all the standing and the sitting, I got confused.

The More Creative
- I was checking to see that the seat bottom was clean and I forgot.
- It was the middle of the night and I had to pee. I wasn't thinking of anything else, I was practically walking in my sleep. I'm lucky I didn't wet the bed.
- I went to an all boys/girls school, and it was never an issue there.
- In my native land, we don't have toilet seats. We squat over a hole in the ground.
- I put the seat up; it must have fallen down during that minor quake.

The Dog
- It's easier for the dog to get a drink when the seat's up.

Social

Forgetting a Name

The Old Standards
- I lost your business card. It was in my wallet when it was stolen.
- I can't remember names—but I never forget a face.
- This always happens when I'm nervous.

The More Creative

- I use word association to remember names, and when I look at you the only words that spring to mind are "cooking oil."
- I'm trained not to remember names. I used to be a secret Communist operative, and they wanted to be sure that if I was ever captured and tortured I wouldn't betray the other members of my cell.
- It's no use—without my social secretary at my side I never have a clue as to who anybody is.
- I'm practicing to play President Ronald Reagan in a historical pageant and I can't recall a thing.
- Hey, I've never seen you before in my life. Oh my God! Where am I? Who am I? Where do I live? Help me. Aaaaaahh!

The Dog

- I keep wanting to call you "Willie" because you remind me of our old dachshund King Wilhelm.

Not Taking Your Car

The Old Standards

- The gas tank is bone dry.
- I drove last time.
- My car's too small—yours has much more room.
- The car has been acting up—it's not very reliable.

The More Creative

- I've been caught speeding so much, the police watch for my car.
- I need to leave the car at home. The insurance adjustor is supposed to come by and appraise the damage from the last accident.
- My insurance doesn't cover passengers.
- If I take my car out of the driveway, thieves will know I'm not home and they'll come by and clean me out.
- I don't want to lose my parking spot.

The Dog
- The dog is shedding and his hair's all over the car seats.

Not Paying the Check at a Restaurant

The Old Standards
- I forgot my wallet/purse.
- Oh my goodness, it looks like I have nothing smaller than a $1,000 bill.
- I don't get paid until tomorrow.
- I'll be right back. I've got to go to the bathroom.

The More Creative
- You don't really expect me to pay for this slop, do you? There was a fly in my soup. I found a roach in the roast, and a mouse in the mousse.
- I'm a food critic. I will, of course, offer to pay for this meal; but I've always found that the better restaurants refuse to accept payment.
- It's my birthday and I assumed you'd all treat me, so I didn't bring any money.
- I've got an idea. You pay this time and I'll pay the next time. It's so much more gracious and it'll give us a reason to get together again.
- I'm a city health inspector and if I pay for this meal, I'll have to put it on my expense report, which means I'll have to inspect the kitchen. Let's just forget I was here today and I'll come back when you're better prepared. Trust me.

The Dog
- I have to get my dog from the vet, and if I pay my share of this bill, I won't have enough money left. Unfortunately, he only takes cash, and if I don't pay in twenty-four hours, he gasses Fru-Fru.

Not Dancing

The Old Standards
- I'm shy.
- I don't know how.
- I'd love to, but I have two left feet.

The More Creative
- I prefer to watch. It's so primal and primitive, like an exercise in anthropology.
- Look at how warped this floor is!
- I get too sexually excited when I dance.
- I'd hate to show off in front of all these lovely people. They are trying so hard.
- I save my energy for real exercise. If I dance now, I'll never be able to run.
- That head injury ruined my equilibrium. When I try to dance, I fall over.
- I was forced to take dancing lessons when I was younger; it was a humiliating experience, and I vowed that I'd never dance again.
- Every time I dance, someone puts on a strobe light, and that triggers my seizures.
- I think that dancing is an intimate thing, not to be done in public.
- The elders of my church forbid dancing.
- I dance for a living. Asking me to dance is like asking a prostitute for a freebie.

The Dog
- I sweat so much when I dance that I attract dogs for miles around.

Using Lame Excuses
[There is no excuse for this.]

Interrupting

The Old Standards
- Excuse me, but I just have to say this before I forget. . . .
- You looked like you were having so much fun over here I just had to join you.
- This will only take a second. . . .
- Let me share this with you. . . .

The More Creative
- Sorry, but I'd rather hear my voice than yours.
- I see no point in letting you talk on when what I have to say will change your mind.
- I can't bear to let you go on and tire out your jaw that way.
- I have to interrupt. It was getting to the point where what you were saying numbed my brain so much it actually made sense.
- Let me affirm what you are saying with this other perspective. . . .
- You're so bright you're losing the audience. Let me say a few things on their level to regain their interest.
- I'm just going to break in every now and then so you can get used to speaking in soundbites.
- I was dying of boredom, so I had to speak up.
- I thought you might want some comments that reflected reality before you got too far into dreamland.
- That was talking? I thought it was just babble. . . .

The Dog
- Sorry to interrupt, but you were taking so long and I have to get back to my dog. Every minute of ours is seven of his, so it really *was* taking a long time.

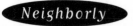
Neighborly

Not Being Neighborly

The Old Standards
- I'm a private person.
- They're the new people—they should make the first move.
- They just don't look like our kind of people.

The More Creative
- I don't want to be friends with my neighbors. If we're friends, they'll be over here all the time and we'll lose all privacy.
- I think we show them more respect if we leave them alone. I never believed in that silly welcome-to-the-neighborhood crap.
- Robert Frost was right: "Good fences make good neighbors."
- I'm very materialistic, and we'll stay on better terms if I don't put myself in a position where they feel welcome to borrow things from me.
- They might turn out to be serial killers. And, if they do, I don't want to have to tell the reporters that "they always seemed quite normal." I'd rather just say I didn't know them.

The Dog
- I don't even want to meet them. After what Nibbs did to their yard, they must hate us already.

Not Returning Something You Borrowed

The Old Standards
- I thought it was a gift.
- I couldn't possibly return it before I've cleaned it.
- I thought my wife/husband/significant other/daughter/son/parole officer/employee returned it.

The More Creative
- It has taken on my aura. It is now part of my soul.
- I'm horribly anal-retentive and it's a problem for me to give up anything.
- It is time for you to start on your path to becoming a monk. You have given up an important material possession. Congratulations.
- I got divorced since I last saw you and my spouse kept it.
- I thought it was a chain-loan. You loaned it to me, I've loaned it to Pete, he loaned it to Neal . . .
- It got damaged and I've ordered a new one to replace it.
- The stars are wrong. I will return it when the astral alignment is better.

The Dog
- After what Spot did to it, I didn't think you'd want it back.

Double Parking

The Old Standards
- I'll only be a minute.
- There's plenty of room for cars to get around me.
- My baby is asleep in the car and I didn't want to wake him/her. I parked her so I could keep an eye on him/her.

The More Creative
- Parallel parking is out of the question. Something's wrong with the transmission and I can't get it into reverse.
- I don't want to take the chance of another car blocking me in.
- I used to rob banks and I guess I haven't gotten that fast-getaway mentality out of my system yet.
- Wow, you're right. I thought I was suffering from double vision.

- I was being followed and double parking is the best way to get the attention of the police.

The Dog
- When I have the dog in the car and park next to the curb, he gets so excited, he goes all over the seat. You see, being civic minded, I taught Fortas to relieve himself at the curb. I guess it's a case of operant conditioning, like Pavlov's dogs, he sees the curb and he defecates: cause and effect. I just got into the habit of double parking, because it keeps him that much further away from the place where he goes to the bathroom.

Not Babysitting a Friend's Children

The Old Standards
- I'd love to, but I'm going to be away then.
- My house isn't childproof.
- The responsibility makes me too nervous.

The More Creative
- Last time I babysat a friend's kids, I lost them in the mall. But I'm willing to give it another shot.
- I'd love to. I especially like changing their diapers and rubbing baby powder all over their cute little tushies. It's so stimulating.
- Having your kids around would upset my boyfriend; he wants to have kids of his own.
- My neighbors are already upset because I take in addicts and illegal aliens. If they see me taking in kids, too, they'll go nuts.
- I'm uncomfortable socializing with anyone who doesn't smoke.
- Great, as long as I can take them along when I see my parole officer.

The Dog
- My babysitting your kids is not a great idea. My pup has a strange case of skin worms and the vet says they're very contagious.

Not Coaching Little League

The Old Standards
- I don't have the time.
- I never understood baseball.
- I don't like kids.

The More Creative
- I refuse to work in any part of this anti-feminist sport. How many women, after all, are in the major leagues?
- It's time the United States gave up on baseball and joined the world community in playing soccer.
- Baseball is bad training for business. No deadlines.
- I think it's just absurd that the team on defense controls the ball.
- I refuse to participate in an activity that rewards stealing!

The Dog
- Every time I bring a mitt home. Fluffy chews it up.

Not Buying Girl Scout Cookies

The Old Standards
- I already bought some from my niece.
- I'm on a diet.
- Sorry, I'm broke.

The More Creative
- I refuse to contribute to the stereotype that females get ahead in this world through baked goods.

- What bad training for motherhood. They should distribute protein, not cookies.
- It's all a big hoax. The girls don't even bake them.
- I'm diabetic.
- No way. I buy the cookies and next thing you know some ambitious DA has me up on charges for giving money to nubile young girls.

The Dog
- Last time I bought cookies the dog ate them all; they nearly killed him.

Not Voting

The Old Standards
- It wouldn't make any difference.
- I don't really like any of the candidates.
- If I vote, they'll have my name and call me for jury duty.

The More Creative
- The voting booth makes me claustrophobic.
- I'm an illegal alien.
- I'm a convicted felon.
- The school where I vote is full of asbestos.
- The voting booth reminds me of a portable toilet.
- Not voting is important. It keeps those clowns from thinking they have a popular mandate.
- Politics is all a sham. There's a secret cabal of permanent bureaucrats who really runs everything.
- I'm afraid I'm not really up on politics. They censored most of the news that came into the ward.

The Dog
- The dog ate my mail-in ballot.

Not Giving to a Charity

The Old Standards
- I gave at the office.
- I have other charities that I support.
- I don't give at this time of year—it's a matter of tax planning.

The More Creative
- You sell raffle tickets. I know. I've seen them. And that's gambling. I will not support any organization that sponsors gambling.
- I was saving some money for you, but the PBS telethon got to me and I gave it to them.
- You'll just take my money and spend it on more mailings asking for more money. And those mailings will use paper, which means killing trees. I'm not about to encourage the deforestation of the earth.
- Ever since Jim and Tammy, I can't see giving to charity. I mean, how do I know you aren't abusing the funds? Seems to me that the devil is choosing to show up as a do-gooder a lot these days.
- I think my first responsibility to charity is to keep myself from needing charity. That's why I'm holding onto my dollars.
- Don't you know that charity is karmically bad for both parties? It sets up a global sort of codependency that engenders bad consequences by violating the Darwinian order. Save yourself; forget charity.

The Dog
- I'm setting up my own charity. When I die, it will support Spot in the style to which he's become accustomed.

Not Serving on Jury Duty

The Old Standards
- The system doesn't work.
- I'd love to, but now's a bad time.
- If I didn't show up at work, my boss would give my job to someone else.

The More Creative
- Who am I to judge someone else?
- I have a medical condition. I can't sit for more than a few moments at a time without having to take a pee.
- The waste in the jury system makes my blood boil, and I can't take the strain.
- I can't agree to follow a judge's instructions. I insist on following my own conscience.
- Sure. And what if I vote to convict someone and they get executed? With my luck, their ghost will materialize out of my TV set and haunt me for the rest of my life.
- I'd love to serve. I have this incredible knowledge of the ways of criminals from reading mystery novels. I know every guilty little trick they use. I dream of hanging some of the thieves and slanderers who are ripping apart the fabric of our fine society.
- I will serve in the name of the Revolution! Once more, we storm the Bastille and set the oppressed free! The cops are the criminals, and all the criminals are saints!
- Can all the testimony be provided via modem? I'd be happy to be a telejuror.

The Dog
- What if I got sequestered on a big trial and couldn't get home to feed my dog Seymour? He won't take food from anyone else.

Not Attending Church/Temple/Mosque

The Old Standards
- I overslept—again.
- It's the only day of the week I get to relax.
- I don't like the church here—I like the one I grew up with.
- By the time I get the kids up, fed, and dressed, the service is over.

The More Creative
- I believe it's sacrilegious to go to church. We must follow God's example and rest on the seventh day.
- I worship at a monastery in Tibet, but the weekly commute would kill me.
- I'm nearsighted, so I prefer to watch the tele-evangelists in the privacy of my own house.
- I'm a communist.
- It conflicts with Little League.

The Dog
- Dog spelled backwards is God.

Not Being on a Committee/ Board/Community-Planning Group/etc.

The Old Standards
- I can't get away from work that early.
- I'd love to, but I'm really just too busy.
- I just don't have the training; that's a task for people with professional backgrounds.

The More Creative
- I'm a nymphomaniac and I always have affairs with the people I work with. It ends up disrupting the whole process.

- I never had much of a family life when I was growing up because my parents were always at committee meetings. I promised myself I wouldn't make the same mistake.
- Basically, I don't believe in that stuff. Pure dictatorship is the only form of government that's ever accomplished anything.
- Sure I'll serve. But let me warn you. My religious convictions are such that I must use any position of authority to benefit my guru.
- I really don't think you want someone with a fatal disease to be part of your group, do you?
- I don't believe in volunteer work. I'm a capitalist. Giving away work subverts the system. Volunteer committees are the hallmark of communism.

The Dog

- Gosh, I'd love to. But all my spare time is devoted to trying to housebreak my dog, General Schwartzkopf. He's three now, and it's about time!

Financial

Not Saving Money

The Old Standards

- Why save? Inflation will wipe out anything we put away.
- It seems pointless to save when interest rates are so low.
- I'll start saving as soon as I get a raise.

The More Creative

- I have a different investment plan. I'm investing in good times. Later, I'll write about them and get rich. It worked for Hemingway and Fitzgerald, didn't it?
- It's absurd to think that you can save enough to make a dif-

ference, given modern medical costs. The best plan is to be broke so you can immediately get help from the government.
- The bomb could wipe us all out, any day. Why save?
- I don't save because I'm planning to work until the day I drop.
- My saving plan is to buy lottery tickets. I'm bound to hit by the time I retire.

The Dog
- Given dog life expectancies, I only have about six years left with Squiffy. I'm spending everything I can to make them great years.

Not Balancing Your Checkbook

The Old Standards
- I'm terrible with numbers.
- It's a joint account and balancing it is my spouse's job.
- I wrote a check and forgot to record it. I can't keep a balance until I find out how much that check was for.

The More Creative
- With all the fees, direct deposits, and added interest these days, it's impossible to keep an accurate balance—so why try?
- My bank takes so long to clear deposits that my numbers and theirs never agree. The only safe way to go is to call them when I want to know my balance.
- If the balance is written in my checkbook, and it's stolen, the thieves will know exactly how much they can forge a check for.
- I don't want to know my balance—it's just too depressing.
- My father balances my checkbook for me when he visits. It makes him feel useful.
- I don't know how to balance my checkbook. My secretary always does it for me.
- As long as I have checks in my checkbook, I must have

money in the bank. Therefore, I don't need to worry about that balancing thing.
- I like to live on the edge.
- I don't keep a balance because I want to tell my ex-wife's lawyer, whenever he calls, that I have no idea how much money I have.
- I'm going to keep my checkbook on my computer, as soon as I learn the program.

The Dog
- The cover of my checkbook is the same color as my dog's favorite toy. Every time I take my checkbook out, Cripps goes right after it; he thinks it's time to play.

Not Using the Automatic Teller Machine (ATM) to Get Money from Your Account

The Old Standards
- I forgot my personal access code.
- It won't let me take any more money out until tomorrow.
- I left my card at home.

The More Creative
- I'm afraid the damn machine will eat my card.
- I'm opposed to automation that puts tellers out of work.
- I can't deal with the beggars who've camped out next to my ATM.
- It's too late to get money out. I'm afraid I might get mugged.
- The cameras they use to monitor the ATM emit harmful radiation.

The Dog
- My dog licked the magnetic strip off the back of my card and the machine refuses to respond.

Being Ignorant of the Stock Market

The Old Standards
- To really understand it you have to work at it full time.
- It's all mumbo jumbo and magic anyway.
- I hate to admit it, but I've never been able to understand fractions.
- That's my broker's job.

The More Creative
- It's pointless. We're due for worldwide depression and a return to the gold standard.
- I'm an artiste, not a number cruncher.
- The big corporations control the stock market. The little guy doesn't have a chance.
- I don't gamble.
- What!? I'd rather be ignorant than deal with slime bags like those takeover artists.
- My astrologer takes care of all that.

The Dog
- My dog does all the investing in our household. Every morning we spread out the stock-quotation section of *The Wall Street Journal* on the kitchen floor, and wait for Tidbit to pee. The mutt's uncanny; we made a killing in wheat futures the other day.

Missing a Bill Payment

The Old Standards
- I never got the bill.
- My check must have gotten lost in the mail.
- I was out of town.
- I mailed the check this morning.
- I spilled coffee on it.

The More Creative
- The bank put my money into the wrong account. They accidentally shipped me some deposit slips with a number for this other guy and, when I used one of them; *my* money went into *his* account. We've just figured it out, but the bank is stalling because the other guy spent the money.
- But I called you and some guy at your office said I could skip a month.
- I just won the lottery and my attorney has forbidden me to pay anything without his approval, so I don't get taken advantage of by opportunists.
- Who am I? I must have amnesia. . . .
- My colostomy bag leaked all over the bills and I had to throw them out.
- They're stealing my mail again. It wasn't enough that they tried to get me with gamma rays—now they need another way to drive me crazy.

The Dog
- All my finances were up on the computer, but it got all screwed up when the dog peed on the socket and blew the fuse.

Having a Junky Car

The Old Standards
- I like old cars—the insurance is lower.
- It may be a wreck, but it's paid for.
- I have to keep the car. It's not paid off yet.

The More Creative
- It's good to have a junky car—no one will ever steal it.
- When I get stopped for speeding, the police feel sorry for me.
- I'll only buy American cars, and this is the last good model Detroit made.

- This way I don't get upset when the car gets dented.
- The only people who drive fancy cars are the nouveau riche and people having midlife crises.
- This car is a shrine. I lost my virginity in it.

The Dog
- I can't have a good car. My dog gets carsick and he'll ruin the upholstery.

Having a Dilapidated Home

The Old Standards
- It's a mess, but it's home.
- We could do better, but we're used to the neighborhood.
- It's the college fund or the house. Which would you choose?

The More Creative
- If we improve the place, it'll make our neighbors' houses look bad.
- If we fix it up, the local tax assessor will just jack up our property taxes.
- Fix up your house, and you become a target for thieves.
- I'm not comfortable with overly fancy places. It feels like I'm putting on airs. I like my home to be humble.
- We'll fix it up when the kids are big enough to help with the work.

The Dog
- Why fix it up when Big Boy is just going to tear up the yard?

Not Being a Millionaire

The Old Standards
- I just didn't get the breaks.
- I was born at the wrong time. The real opportunities for entrepreneurs like me are all gone.

- What's the point of being rich anymore? The government just takes it all in taxes.

The More Creative
- I have focused on spiritual, not material, rewards.
- I could have become rich, but then I would have had to worry about kidnapping all the time.
- I purposely stay poor, because the richer I get, the more money my ex-spouse gets.
- I could have become a millionaire, but I refused to sell out. True artists are poor.
- I wouldn't want to be a millionaire—rich people have such screwed-up kids.
- I should be a millionaire, but I was too trusting. I got ripped off by my broker.

The Dog
- I once had a winning lottery ticket, but the dog ate it.

two

Individual

Not Going to the Doctor

The Old Standards
- The pain isn't that bad.
- I can't take the time off of work.
- I know what my problem is—I just don't eat right.

The More Creative
- I view my body spiritually, as a temple. I don't want it violated by some cold, unfeeling, unbelieving scientist.
- Doctors' offices are as likely to do harm as good. They are full of all sorts of sick people with all those germs. I'll probably catch something worse there.
- I'm doing my part to keep national health care costs down.
- My grandmother never went to the doctor and she lived to be ninety-seven.
- I think all doctors are control freaks.

- Sometimes doctors don't tell you what they're doing and inject you with strange stuff and use you as a subject for their bizarre experiments.
- I believe my body can cure itself—it's a holistic thing.
- I'm not afraid of the doctor, but I can't handle all the insurance forms.

The Dog
- The doctor will just tell me I'm allergic to my dog, and I won't get rid of him.

Not Going to the Dentist

The Old Standards
- I can't take the pain.
- My insurance doesn't cover it, and I can't afford to go right now.
- I was planning to go, but something came up at work and I had to cancel my appointment.

The More Creative
- No way. I made the mistake of renting "Marathon Man" last night.
- Since I floss every day, I don't need to go to the dentist.
- I'm not going until they wrap up that awful case about the AIDS-infected dentist.
- I have a heart murmur, and my doctor told me I need to be careful when having my teeth checked because a major source of blood is located near the mouth. One slip of a dentist's instruments could cause excessive bleeding which, in turn, could force my heart to go into some kind of shock and lead to a massive coronary. You can understand that I don't want to take any chances.
- I read that those x-rays they force you to have can cause cancer.

The Dog
- My dog doesn't go to any dentist, and his teeth are fine. Why should I?

Not Having a Will

The Old Standards
- I hate thinking about death.
- I have no one to leave my stuff to, anyway.
- I'm too young to think about dying.

The More Creative
- I don't care what happens after I'm gone. Why should I?
- Whatever kind of will I create, it will give someone motivation to kill me. Why risk it?
- I'm Darwinian. I want my heirs to fight it out when I'm gone. And may the fittest triumph!
- Who needs a will? I'm spending it all and leaving only debts.
- I'm using my own process for creating a will. Anyone who asks me about the will gets cut out. Thanks for eliminating yourself.
- Wills are bad for your karma. They make you try and control a process when you should be letting go.

The Dog
- My first instinct is to leave everything to the dog. But I know that's stupid. I just can't make up my mind.

Buying New Clothes

The Old Standards
- Everything I have is out of style.
- Everyone at the party has already seen my other outfits.
- It cheers me up to go shopping.

- Do you want your boss to see me in a shabby outfit? He'll think you spend all our money on booze.
- When I'm dead and buried, I'll wear the same outfit forever. While I'm alive, I want some variety.
- I'm testing to see who knows the real me, and who knows me by my outfits.
- How do you expect us to get rich? Money only comes to the people who look wealthy.
- I just lost five pounds and I want something that shows off the new me.
- I already feel bad enough because I gained five pounds and have to buy new clothes. Don't make me feel any worse.
- I work very hard to maintain my weight. I should be rewarded for that; not punished by being made to wear the same outfit all the time.
- Dressing is my artistic outlet. Think of clothes as my art supplies.
- I read someplace that shopping for clothes is the perfect aerobic workout.
- You don't want me to look good anymore! Are you going out with someone else?
- All those old clothes remind me of people I went out with before I met you.

The Dog

- I had to buy new clothes after what the dog did to my old ones.

Not Buying New Clothes

The Old Standards

- I like my old clothes. They're comfortable.
- Waste not, want not.
- My old stuff is just coming back into style.

The More Creative
- There is so much change in my life. My clothes are the one thing I can keep constant.
- I'm thinking of moving, and I want to buy clothes appropriate to my new home, once I find it.
- When I dress well, people try to sell me stuff. As long as I look like a bum, they leave me alone.
- They use all sorts of noxious chemicals when they manufacture clothes these days. It's a good idea to avoid wearing new clothes whenever you can.
- I'm planning on losing some weight. It would be demoralizing to buy new clothes, and then have to get rid of them when I change size.
- New clothes are a vanity. Look to the lilies of the field. Does not the Lord clothe them in beauty?

The Dog
- The dog's eyesight is not too good and he relies on smell. If I got new clothes I'd smell different, and that would confuse him.

Returning Merchandise

The Old Standards
- It's the wrong size.
- We already have two of these.
- It's the wrong color.
- Neither of us will ever learn how to use it.

The More Creative
- Our lease prohibits our having any of these.
- We have an infant in the house, and a (fill in item)'s just not appropriate for a baby.
- My husband and I are missionaries and the Lord has called

us to go and spread His word in Mauritania. We have to travel light, so there is no way we can bring a (<u>fill in name of item</u>) with us.
- We've won the lottery and can afford to shop at Neiman Marcus now.
- It interferes with our TV reception.

The Dog
- My dog's allergic to it.

Watching TV All the Time

The Old Standards
- I'm not just watching TV; I'm doing other things at the same time.
- There's nothing else to do.
- I'm only watching the educational stations.

The More Creative
- Where do you think I learned to cook like this?
- What's wrong with watching TV? It's not the "idiot box" it was when you were a kid. Today, it's more like an informational highway and stuff like that.
- I'm a modern day cultural historian and the TV is the best way for me to see life as it really is without leaving the comfort of my living room.
- I work hard so I can watch hard.
- Don't blame me, blame ESPN/HBO/Showtime/CNN.

The Dog

- I don't have the TV on for me, I have it on for my dog. He loves the constant chatter.

Not Taking Pictures

The Old Standards
- The camera's packed all the way in the bottom of my suitcase.
- I forgot to buy film/bring camera.
- It's too much of a hassle, and I have no idea how the flash works.

The More Creative
- Cameras steal your soul.
- Photography is a nasty chemical process. Do you have any idea what silver halides do to an aquifer?
- Once you put a camera in front of you, you're removed from the situation. I want to experience *everything* directly, without mediation.
- Photography is all about saving the past. I want to live in the present.
- Cameras always make people self-conscious. They kill spontaneity.
- You never know when someone is going to switch your camera with one of those gun cameras that spies use.
- I was a correspondent once in a divorce suit that involved the lawyer for the other side talking about a pile of black and white photographs taken by a detective. Ever since that, I've not been too excited about photography.

The Dog
- My dog ate my film, but it's okay, nothing developed.

Bad Handwriting

The Old Standards
- I just don't have the coordination.
- I was born a lefty, but the nuns forced me to write with my right hand.
- Good handwriting is for girls.

The More Creative
- I'm a thinker, not a packager. I care about the content—not what it looks like.
- Handwriting is doomed, anyway. In a few years we will all be dictating to computers.
- The junta broke my hands, but they cannot stop me from writing!
- All those early years working in the meat packing plant have taken their toll; I have horrible arthritis.
- It's code. No one can read it except me.
- I always wanted to be a doctor. I never made it to medical school, but at least I have the handwriting.

The Dog
- The dog chewed up all my pens—all I have left are the refills, and they're real tough to write with.

Procrastinating
[NOTE: The authors can't think of any excuses right now. We'll try to get back to this section later.]

Personal Appearance

Being Fat

The Old Standards
- I have no will power.
- It was either eat the apple pie or hurt my mother's feelings.
- It's a genetic problem.

The More Creative
- I retain more water than most.
- I'm on a special antipsychotic medication and this is one of the side effects.

- I'm up for the role of Falstaff in Shakespeare's *The Merry Wives of Windsor.*
- I'm not fat, the cleaner shrunk my clothes.
- I'm only fat if you believe all that hype you hear from the fashion industry.
- I don't want my friends to think I'm HIV positive.

The Dog
- My dog has tapeworms and is eating constantly. Unfortunately, he hates to eat alone.

Being Thin

The Old Standards
- I've been sick.
- Thin! You think I'm thin? Just look at this gut.
- I metabolize my food quicker than most people.
- I work out a lot.

The More Creative
- I travelled extensively in the third world and picked up an odd assortment of parasites.
- I'm a model, it's my job to be thin.
- I want to be a TV star, and I read some place that TV adds ten pounds to your appearance.
- I'm not really that thin; I wear very baggy clothes.
- I'm fasting in solidarity with the people in (<u>fill in the name of a currently oppressed country</u>.)
- I *love* to puke!

The Dog
- My dog gets to the food faster than I do.

Being Bald

The Old Standards
- There was nothing I could do about it, my mother's father was bald.
- I think it looks sexy.
- It's a hormonal thing.

The More Creative
- I was in a terrible accident when I was young, but I don't want to talk about it.
- I'm on the swim team. I shaved my head because the hair was slowing me down.
- I volunteered for a psychopharmacology experiment and I neglected to read the fine print.
- I'm not bald. My head has been fitted with the latest, very expensive, custom-made solar sex panel.
- I was an Easter egg in the village pageant.
- It's a reaction to the chemotherapy. Thank you for asking.

The Dog
- I usually wear a toupee, but my pooch thought it was one of those Maltese dogs and tried to mate with it.

Having Bad Hair

The Old Standards
- My mirror's broken.
- It's "bed head." I went to sleep when it was still wet.
- My hat ruined my hairdo—I have hat hair.

The More Creative
- The reason my hair looks so bad is because I combed it in the dark; my electricity is out.

- I've got more important things to do than worry about my hair.
- My no-longer-employed hairdresser said, "Trust me."
- I took the kids to the science museum, and made the mistake of volunteering to take part in some stupid static-electricity experiment.
- My hair always does this when I've just seen a ghost.
- Shows what little you know. This is the latest in hair fashion out of Milan.
- I felt if I walked around with my hair looking like this, my kids would be embarrassed enough to make sure theirs was properly coiffed.
- An Oprah special came on in the middle of my haircut and the barber paid more attention to the TV than to my head.

The Dog
- I own a sheep dog, and you know what they say about dogs and their masters starting to look like each other.

Not Wearing Any Makeup

The Old Standards
- I overslept and didn't have time to put any on.
- Makeup is so unnatural.
- I'm allergic to most cosmetics; I have very sensitive skin.
- My parents don't approve of makeup.

The More Creative
- I read about how they test cosmetics on cute little bunnies and swore never to wear makeup ever again.
- It is so warm out, I thought it would just drip off my face.
- If someone's going to love me, they're going to love me for myself, not my makeup.
- It's against my religion.

- I'm bummed out.
- I'm going to ask for a raise later today and I want to look like I've really been working hard.
- I broke up with my boyfriend.
- I'm waiting until after my workout.
- Why bother? There's no one here I need to look good for.
- I'll start wearing makeup when I reach your age.
- I'm on my way to my parent's house.
- So, what are you saying, you think I need to wear makeup?

The Dog
- Every time I put on makeup, my dog starts barking and he won't stop.

Wearing Too Much Makeup

The Old Standards
- The light was bad.
- You don't want to see what I look like without it.
- I guess it's a generational thing. You kids today look like you just got out of bed.
- There is no such thing as too much makeup.

The More Creative
- I'm doing my Tammy Faye Bakker impersonation.
- I put it on thick because it has to last all day.
- It looks heavy in normal light, but it's perfect for TV lighting.
- I forgot to pack my own makeup and had to use my mother's.
- I was in a terrible car accident and I need to wear this much makeup in order to cover my hideous scars.
- I'm trying to hide an unusually virulent case of acne.
- I always wanted to join a circus and be a clown, but I had other responsibilities. This is my way of compensating.
- What makeup?!

The Dog
- It's the only thing I can do to keep my boyfriend's dog from licking my face—dog germs, yuuck!

Having a Run in Your Pantyhose

The Old Standards
- I didn't notice it until I was out of the house.
- I caught my leg on the car door while I was getting out.
- There's a screw or something sticking out of the bottom of my desk.

The More Creative
- My husband used my good hose as an air filter for the dryer.
- My son has a leg injury and he's been wearing my hose under his football pants.
- I came home during a robbery and the thief put my hose over his head so I couldn't identify him.
- My daughter used my good hose to strain some gravy.
- My grandson took my hose and made a minnow net out of them.
- I just had my fingernails tipped and I didn't realize how long and how sharp they were. I put my fingers right through the hose when I put them on.
- Get with it. Ripped hose is a fashion look, just like ripped jeans.
- I was using the rest room in a gas station. Of course, it was filthy, the stall door had no lock, and there was a puddle on the floor. I squatted to stay off the seat, used one arm to hold the door shut and the other to keep the crotch of the pantyhose above the puddle. But when I was through, I had to let go of the door to reach the paper, and the door swung in and ripped the hose.

The Dog
- My sister's stupid dog jumped up on my leg.

Not Having Intercourse

The Old Standards
- I have a headache.
- It's that time of the month.
- I'm not in the mood.
- I love you, but you're like a brother/sister to me.

The More Creative
- When I was little, I saw two horses having sex. Of course, I had no idea what they were doing, but the act was so violent and frenzied I can't get that terrible image out of my head. It was very traumatic. You understand, don't you?
- My leather corset is at the cleaners.
- The planets are not in the proper alignment.
- I thought our relationship was on a much higher plane.
- I'd like to make love with you. Would you mind if I called you "Mommy"?
- I think I have herpes, but it's okay with me if it's okay with you.

The Dog
- I just can't right now. It's too close to the death of my dog, and I don't want this to be a rebound thing.

Not Using a Condom

The Old Standards
- They cut out all the sensations that make sex really good.
- They ruin the mood.
- I'm too embarrassed to buy them.

The More Creative
- They don't have my size.
- I thought you would take a condom as an insult—like it

implied you might have loose morals and have slept around and caught all sorts of diseases.

- I just read in the papers that the condoms I usually use have been recalled. Turns out some angry ex-employee had snuck into the factory and punctured hundreds of thousands of cases of condoms with a tiny pin. So what's the point of using one?
- My nephew was over the other day and discovered my stash of condoms. I found him and his friends up on the roof; they had turned all my condoms into water balloons and were dropping them on the people as they walked by.
- I'm allergic to latex.

The Dog

- I used an entire box of condoms last night. You see, I took the dog with me to the pharmacy, and on our way home he decided to take a dump. I was so pissed. I had forgotten to bring the dog's pooper scooper. I looked around for something to pick up the mess with, but found nothing. Then I had a brainstorm. I opened all the condoms—I had a box of 10—and put one on each finger. I picked all up his poop and deposited it in the appropriate receptacle. Unfortunately, I didn't have enough money on me to buy another box.

Not Having an Orgasm

The Old Standards

- I don't know what the problem is.
- I thought I heard someone outside the door.
- I guess I'm just too tense.
- Look at the time! I've got to go.

The More Creative

- I didn't want to get your sheets wet.
- I guess I was more concerned that you got off.

- I'm saving myself for later.
- It's not my fault. It's just that my last lover was so much bigger.
- I was so close. Why did you stop?
- That's okay—it was nice anyway.
- When I was in school, I volunteered for a psychological experiment involving orgasms. I was in the group that got an electric shock each time we came. I guess I haven't gotten over anticipating the pain.
- I was in 'Nam and I was exposed to Agent Orange. I think my sperm is toxic and I don't want to infect you.
- I'm not really that liberated—I've never gotten past feeling that sex is dirty.

The Dog
- Whenever I come, I scream really loudly and that upsets my dog. He starts barking and doesn't stop. You don't know how many times the neighbors have called to complain.

Not Getting an Erection

The Old Standards
- I'm drunker than I thought.
- This never happened before.
- I think the kids are still awake.

The More Creative
- I can't get the concept of world hunger out of my head.
- It's just too cold in here.
- After all those years of worrying about getting someone pregnant, the damned trouser trout has become conditioned to being flaccid.
- It's kinky, but I just can't get it up with someone who doesn't mistreat me.
- If only you hadn't worn those full-cut panties—they remind me of my mother.

The Dog
- It's the damn dog's fault. He won't stop staring at me.

Getting an Erection at an Inopportune Time

The Old Standards
- It's got a mind of its own.
- Sorry.
- I'm so embarrassed.

The More Creative
- That's not an erection, I've got an banana in my pocket.
- I was thinking about the time a friend showed me his pictures from the nudist colony.
- Thank God it still works, I've been so nervous lately.
- I bought some new underwear; it's ribbed and sometimes rubs me the wrong way. (Or is that the right way?)
- I suffer from priapism.
- It's a side-effect of the medication I'm taking.
- My body got so used to saltpeter in the army that when I don't have a lot of it in my diet, I'm erect all the time.

The Dog
- We live in a society of double standards. No one makes a big deal when a dog sports a boner in public.

Premature Climax

The Old Standards
- I'm just not used to anyone as sexy as you are.
- That's never happened before.
- I thought you had come already.

The More Creative
- It's just that it's been so long since I last had sex. I've been waiting for a special partner, like you.
- It's a holdover from prison. Getting caught in the act there is deadly, so you learn to come fast.
- I didn't want to go on for hours and tire you out.
- What did you do to make me do that?
- Hey, isn't it time for Letterman?
- I'm not a control freak.

The Dog
- It's natural. That's how dogs do it—the point is to come.

Not Having Oral Sex

The Old Standards
- It's just too gross, yuck.
- I'm not that kind of girl/boy.
- I don't know you well enough.

The More Creative
- It's not a good idea. I have these seizures that cause jaw spasms.
- I hate having sex when I can't see your face.
- I hate snakes.
- I have a very sensitive gag reflex.
- I went to the zoo when I was six and as we walked by the gorilla's cage, the big ape threw a long, erect peeled banana and it hit my baby brother in the face. He had to be rushed to the nearest hospital. Part of the banana was lodged in his nose. For some reason, I can't get that image out of my head.
- I don't mind the taste, but I hate the view.
- I've already eaten, thank you anyway.
- I'd love to, but it's allergy season, and I'm all stuffed up.
- I suffer from lockjaw.

56

The Dog
- I don't lick genitals—that's what dogs do.

Always Thinking/Talking About Sex

The Old Standards
- I can't help it, it's my hormones.
- I'm just articulating what most people are thinking anyway.
- I do not. You're just too much of a prude.

The More Creative
- My role on this planet is to procreate.
- If the skyscrapers weren't so phallic, and the Capitol building is one giant breast . . .
- I'm telepathic and I'm picking up thoughts from others. And let me tell you, there are a lot of people thinking about sex as we speak.
- This isn't excessive—this is normal sexuality. Guess you haven't been exposed to any for quite a while.
- Thinking about sex is merely my way to avoid contemplating the threat of nuclear destruction.
- If I didn't I'd probably be telling you about my work as an actuary. You wouldn't want that, now would you?
- I'm not normally this way—you drive me to it, you wild thing.
- I'm doing research for my novel.

The Dog
- My dog's in heat and he's humping everything in sight. I'm just trying to relate to him through this difficult time.

Infidelity

The Old Standards
- I was drunk.
- He/She meant nothing to me.

- I was thinking of you the whole time.
- I was angry at you.
- I was just trying to get your attention.
- You don't really understand me.

The More Creative
- I know I haven't satisfied you lately and I was trying to see if I could learn something new.
- I thought if I did it just once and got it out of my system, our marriage would be stronger.
- I just have no control over myself during a full moon.
- I was curious. I wanted to see if all men/women were the same.
- It was a fraternity rush requirement.
- It was dark. I thought it was you.
- I thought *you* had been unfaithful and I wanted to hurt you as much as you hurt me.
- I felt that if I was still attractive to other people it would make me more attractive to you.
- He told me if I didn't, he would die. Something about sperm backup . . . I don't know; it was so medical.
- I don't believe in divorce.

The Dog
- She/He threatened to sic the dog on me if I didn't do it.

Getting Pregnant

The Old Standards
- He said he was going to pull out.
- He said he had a vasectomy.
- She said she was wearing a diaphragm.
- It will save our marriage.

The More Creative
- I'm just so powerful I keep bursting the condoms.
- Now we don't have to worry about birth control.

- I swear I'm a virgin. This must be a holy child!
- I know you. Deep in your heart you want a child—it's the only thing that will make you commit.
- It's finally happened. His sperm has become resistant to spermicides!
- My mother was over last month. She must have put pinholes in the condoms. She'll do anything to have grandchildren.

The Dog
- I'm doing it because my dog can't have puppies and her therapist says she'll continue to be depressed until she has something to care for.

Trying Something Kinky

The Old Standards
- I needed to know if I was missing something.
- How can I say I don't like it if I don't try it?
- I read that it will spice up our sex life.
- C'mon. We're an adventurous generation. We don't want to be just like our parents.

The More Creative
- That's not kinky—it's something I saw watching Olympic gymnastics.
- It's important to me that you and I share something that I didn't share with my first spouse.
- I'm writing a book about decadence. I must do research!
- I'm going to hell anyway; I might as well have something different to talk about there.
- My therapist suggested it.

The Dog
- I want to do it for the same reason that a dog licks his balls—because I can!

Vices

Getting Drunk

The Old Standards
- I'm drowning my sorrows.
- I need to relax.
- I didn't know there was alcohol in the punch.
- I'd skipped lunch so I was drinking on an empty stomach.

The More Creative
- I'm on chemotherapy, so my resistance is low.
- I'm only doing what my parents taught me.
- They were trying to get me drunk so they could take advantage of me.
- I have to drink so I can forget the tragedy of the fall of the Roman Empire.
- I'm part Indian, and we Indians don't metabolize alcohol well.
- Drinking is the only way I get to see the world the way less intelligent people do.
- I wanted to piss a lot so I could try and pass a kidney stone.
- I thought that if I drank a lot I could write like Dylan Thomas—he was a great writer and a great drinker.
- You've got to drink a lot to get the taste of oral sex out of your mouth.
- I gave blood today, so I'm a pint low.

The Dog
- Drinking lowers your IQ, and I figured that after nine drinks maybe I could finally understand my old, fleabag mutt, Stanley.

Taking Drugs

The Old Standards
- My doctor prescribed this—really.
- I'm trying to expand my mind.
- It's the only way to deal with this messed-up world we live in.

The More Creative
- I'm not high on drugs; I'm high on life.
- I think it's the least we can do for Southeast Asia—I mean we bombed the hell out of all those countries, so I think we owe it to them to contribute to their high-profit cash crops of coca leaves, poppies, and hemp.
- I missed Woodstock, but I can still live the lifestyle!
- Drugs are the only way I know I haven't sold out.
- I need to have the drug experience so I'll have something in common with my kids.
- I take 'em, but I don't inhale.
- Self-medication is the only way to have humanistic self-control. Otherwise you let yourself fall into the clutches of the German-tradition trained, knife-happy, money-sucking medical profession.

The Dog
- The ability to use drugs is what separates us human from our dogs.

Smoking

The Old Standards
- Give me a break, I started when I was twelve.
- Smoking relaxes me.
- There's no real evidence, outside of hospitals, graveyards, and laboratories, that tobacco causes cancer.

The More Creative
- It's a neurosis. I need something to do with my mouth and hands. If I can't smoke, what alternatives do you have to offer?
- What about the smell? It's better than most perfumes and I don't hear you trying to outlaw them.
- Okay, outlaw tobacco and perfumes, but if you really worry

about smells, first get the French to bathe. You think natural is good, try inhaling on the Paris Metro.
- This great country of ours was built on the blood, sweat, and tears of our tobacco industry. Outlaw cigarettes, and you outlaw history.
- I hate myself.
- I happen to enjoy bothering people with my secondary smoke.
- Look, I need to have at least one vice so people don't think I'm perfect and start to worship me.
- My great-grandmother smoked two packs a day since she was four, and she lived to be 120.
- I find that smoking is an effective way to repel wimps and do-gooders.
- I don't think of it as smoking. In my religion, it's just a personal form of incense.
- What separates us from animals is our conquest of fire. Carrying controlled fire with you is the mark of a truly evolved creature.
- I regard smoking as my contribution to all those poverty areas in the South. Without tobacco, they'd have to eat rocks.
- I associate sex with smoking. It was always that way in the movies I grew up on. Anyway, if I can't smoke, I can't get it up.

The Dog
- I have to smoke to cover up the smell of Fido's farts.

Gambling

The Old Standards
- I just do it for fun. I know when to stop.
- I know what I'm doing, I have a system.
- I'm lucky.

The More Creative
- This is the only honest way to get money. Totally random. No one is exploited. No one is hurt.
- My horoscope said today's the day.
- My shrink said I need more risk in my life.
- There's no way we're going to get ahead with just our salaries. This is really our only chance.
- Gambling helps me think. Something about the adrenalin.
- I had a vision. I am blessed by God. I can't lose.
- I think all white people owe it to the remaining American Indians to spend some money on the reservations.

The Dog
- I won my dog in a card game, and he's the best friend I have. I figure that if I keep gambling, I might win a nice wife/husband.

Overeating

The Old Standards
- I'm always hungry.
- My eyes are bigger than my stomach.
- My mother always made us eat everything on our plates.
- I'm starting my diet tomorrow.

The More Creative
- I have hungry fat cells.
- I paid for it—damnit, I'm going to eat it.
- If we just leave it around, we'll get all sorts of ants and roaches around here. It's better to finish it off.
- There are starving people in India, for God's sake—who are we to turn this down.
- My therapist says it's an oral thing.
- I know how compulsive you are and I'm just trying to save you from having to deal with crumbs and leftovers.

* The ways we store leftovers are so unecological—all that plastic and aluminum foil. It's better for the earth if I eat it all now.

The Dog
* My dog is overweight. If I leave stuff, she gets it, and the vet said no more leftovers.

Lying

The Old Standards
* I didn't want to hurt his/her feelings.
* It was only a little white lie. I didn't mean to hurt anybody.
* No one's going to find out.

The More Creative
* He/She is emotionally unstable, the truth could take him/her right over the edge.
* I wasn't lying, I remember *exactly* what position I was in at the time; I was *sitting* demurely on the settee with my legs crossed.
* I was a counterintelligence officer in the army. It was my job as chief propagandist to disseminate misinformation to the enemy. My ability to lie effectively saved lives. What did *you* do for this country, you commie bastard?
* I was not lying. I was merely withholding specific information I deemed irrelevant to the situation.
* I'm saving the truth for my memoirs.
* I'm a writer, and I was just practicing my ability to create fiction.
* The truth is too complex. I told them something they could understand.

The Dog
* Rick thinks he's human, so I do my best not to use the words "dog," "canine," or "mutt" in front of him. I guess I'm so used to lying in front of him that I end up lying to everyone.

Reading Pornography

The Old Standards
- I read it for the articles.
- I thought I was buying the *Sports Illustrated* swimsuit issue.
- Someone's got to support the free expression of ideas.

The More Creative
- I'm a cultural anthropologist and these publications tell us a lot about our culture.
- All those fit bodies inspire me to keep working out.
- I'm against this kind of stuff, but I feel I need to experience it before I can criticize it.
- I'm trying to get my hormone level up so I can produce more sperm and we can have a baby.
- My grandfather read it, my father read it, and I read it. It's a family tradition.

The Dog
- The dog ate all my good books.

Criminal

Cheating on Taxes

The Old Standards
- Everyone does it.
- I overpaid last year, and I'm evening it out.
- I need the money more than the bureaucrats do.

The More Creative
- I refuse to give money to a government that pays hundreds of dollars for a hammer.
- Cheating on taxes is a subversive act. You deprive the gov-

ernment of the funds to finance repression, and you do it anonymously, so you don't become a target.
- Cheating on taxes is part of my ethnic heritage. Everyone in my home country does it. I must be true to my roots.
- Richard Nixon cheated, why shouldn't I?
- We all cheat in different ways. Some buy politicians and have them create loopholes. I'm just taking a more direct route.

The Dog
- I really meant to pay all my taxes, but the dog ate my records, and I had to guesstimate.

Opening Someone Else's Mail

The Old Standards
- I thought it was for me.
- I thought you said, "What's mine is yours."
- I thought it might be important, and I was going to call you and tell you about it so you'd get the news faster.

The More Creative
- I thought I heard something ticking.
- I'm with the FBI—it's my job.
- I thought it was a bill, and I was going to surprise you by paying it for you.
- It's your fault. Ever since you lied to me, I can't trust you, and I have to do things like open your mail.
- I'm just trying to show some interest in you and what you do, but you make it so hard. It would be much easier if you would talk to me about what you are doing and feeling. But no, I have to open your mail just to get hints.

The Dog
- The dog drooled all over it and I had to open it so the insides wouldn't get smeary and illegible.

Getting Arrested

The Old Standards
- I was framed.
- It was a mistake.
- The sheriff has a vendetta against me.

The More Creative
- I'm always getting arrested for things done by my evil twin.
- I'm a secret news reporter. I'm going inside to get the real story on our prisons.
- The cops have been given quotas and they're making all of these bogus busts.
- I'm being harassed by the government because I'm an independent thinker and speak my mind.
- All the greats have been arrested. Martin Luther King, Gandhi, Mandela . . .
- All I did was refuse to buy a ticket to the policeman's ball.
- Like Thoreau, one must get arrested every now and again in order to maintain perspective.
- Someone stole my wallet a few years ago and used my I.D. to rob and steal. Ever since then I've been arrested for all sorts of things I didn't do.

The Dog
- My dog impregnated the top mutt in the K-9 squad, and that upset the police, so they arrest me every chance they get.

Stealing

The Old Standards
- I was going to come back and pay for it.
- I got cheated at this store last week and I'm only evening the score.
- It was just a prank.

The More Creative
- You mean this isn't a free sample?
- Property is theft! I was liberating it! Things have souls; they want to be in a home, not some big impersonal store.
- Oh, Jesus. You mean to tell me *that* personality is back? The doctor said I was cured . . . but I guess we're not.
- This isn't stealing; it's pacifistic looting. I get the stuff, and you suffer no broken windows. Better for everyone, don't you think?
- Yes, thank you. I wanted you to catch me. Don't you understand what it's like to have a war between good and bad in you? Punishment will be a relief. Thank God I've been stopped.
- It's all part of my psychology training for my masters in social work. They insist we know what it feels like to be a criminal. My professor made me do it!
- This isn't for me. It's for the poor. I'm a modern Robin Hood. Want to see my tights?
- Congratulations. I'm one of the investigators from the retailers' association assigned to survey security in retail establishments throughout the country. Your techniques for tracking unauthorized inventory depletion deserve commendation. Who do you report to?

The Dog
- I meant to pay, but I ran out when I suddenly remembered it was my turn to walk the dog. I was supposed to have him outside two hours ago. The carpet's probably ruined by now.

Speeding

The Old Standards
- Everyone else was driving fast, too.
- Gee, was I really going that fast? My speedometer must be broken.

- I was late and in a hurry.
- What speed limit sign?

- I'm a volunteer fireman and I was going to a fire.
- I'm having my period (NOTE: Men should try the diarrhea version of this excuse) and I really need to get to a rest stop.
- I feel safer when I'm out in front of the traffic.
- I drive a big car so I can speed and still be safe.
- The speed limit is for bad weather. This is a perfectly clear day.
- The cruise control got stuck.
- I forgot which pedal was the accelerator and which was the brake.
- It was the music on the radio. I was driving to the beat.
- I had to escape the Klingons!
- Did you ever stop to think that "speed limit" is an oxymoron?

The Dog
- My dog saw another dog on the street and he would have leapt out of the car and killed himself if I hadn't sped up.

Murder

The Old Standards
- I was temporarily insane.
- It was him or me.
- I was just trying to scare him; I didn't think the gun was loaded.

The More Creative
- I was on a sugar high—the junk food made me do it.
- I was hypnotized by electronic violence.
- I *vas chust* following orders.

- I was abused by him in a former lifetime. This was karmic justice, and it can only be judged on the astral plane.
- It's society's fault. I was sent to 'Nam and trained and paid to kill. Now you punish me for doing it. Well, it's not so easy to deprogram a person.
- It's part of my qualification exam for joining the Postal Workers' Union.
- She had been possessed. Killing her was the only way to free her from Satan.

The Dog

- Sam, the dog, told me to do it.

three

At Home

Domestic

Not Cleaning the Bathroom

The Old Standards
- I was going to do it.
- It's not my turn.
- The smell of (fill in favorite cleanser) stings my nose.

The More Creative
- I can't stand the acoustics. All the noise bounces off the walls and deafens me.
- I wanted to wait until it was dry so I wouldn't slip and hurt myself.
- I'm claustrophobic.
- I haven't had my shots yet. Do you have any idea what kind of deadly germs live around the inside lip of the toilet bowl?
- I'm getting ready for a trip to France and I want to get used to things smelling like a sewer.

- I have a bad back and I can't bend over to clean the tub or the toilet bowl.
- We're trying out a new maid next week and I want that room to be good and dirty, so we get our money's worth.

The Dog
- It *was* clean. I'll bet someone left the toilet seat up and Stubens slurped the water out of the bowl and tracked his filthy paw prints all over the floor.

Not Doing the Laundry

The Old Standards
- I'm out of quarters for the laundromat.
- I needed to buy more underwear, anyway.
- I'm waiting until I have enough clothes for a full load.

The More Creative
- No sense in doing the laundry until I bring my workout clothes home from the gym.
- I'm saving my laundry up until I visit my parents. Nobody folds like my mother.
- After I separate the whites, the colors, the delicates, and the permanent press, the washer's only a quarter full; it's not worth wasting water, soap, and electricity on such small loads.
- I'm waiting until after the exterminator comes. I'll have to wash everything then, anyway, because the fallout from that poison settles over every article of clothing and all the linen in the house.
- I'm waiting until there's a really good movie on TV, so I have something to watch while I'm waiting for the end of the spin cycle.
- I don't know which of your things go into the dryer and which ones have to be hung up to dry.
- I'm planning to do the laundry the night before our trip so I have lots of clean clothes to pack.

The Dog
- I can't do the laundry until I have time to fold it and put it all away. If I leave the laundry out, the dog uses it for a bed. I have to wash everything all over again.

Not Having a Maid

The Old Standards
- We can't afford it.
- My place isn't big enough to warrant a maid.
- I don't trust anybody else to be as thorough as I am.

The More Creative
- I'm not about to perpetuate a service which demeans another individual. I can clean up after myself, thank you.
- I had a maid once, but she robbed me blind while I was at work. Never again.
- My mom lives close by; she does a much better job than any maid could.
- Do you know how much time I'd spend cleaning up the place each time before she arrived?
- I don't trust anyone around my prized art and porcelain collections. Do you have any idea how much it would cost to replace that one-of-a-kind Ming vase if some incompetent maid knocked it over?

The Dog
- My dog is very antisocial and extremely territorial; he ate the last maid.

Having a Maid

The Old Standards
- Everyone I know has one.
- The place is just too big for one person to keep clean.

- I work sixty hours a week, and I just don't have the time to do it myself.

The More Creative
- I'm allergic to an ingredient that is in all household cleansers.
- I figure having a really clean house increases my chances of snagging a spouse.
- I'm so lonely. I don't get out of the house much and I look forward to some companionship.
- I'm doing what I can to help all those illegal aliens get work and start a new life. Don't worry, I'm not planning on running for any public office.
- I'm not paying for it, my parents are.
- I won a contest and this was the first prize: maid service for life.
- I live in such a remote area that I like the idea of someone coming over regularly. Who else will find me if I slip and fall?
- Maybe my husband will leave me alone now.
- I went to college so I wouldn't have to do the cleaning.
- If we had to rely on my cleaning skills, the social worker would say the place was unsafe for the kids.
- I want the house to be spotless, in case someone from "60 Minutes" comes over to interview me.

The Dog
- Jeepers hates to be left alone. I tried to placate him with the TV and radio, but he could tell the difference. This way he has someone to keep him company, and I get my house cleaned at the same time.

Not Doing the Grocery Shopping

The Old Standards
- I went last time.
- We've got plenty of food in the house.
- I lost the list.

The More Creative

- There's a rumor going around that someone's tampering with boxes and cans at the grocery stores in the area. Something about the threat of poison.
- I spent too many years in the Soviet Union, and I can't deal with American abundance.
- I think the boy who bag the groceries is wanted for murder. It's not worth putting my life on the line for a box of chocolate chip cookies.
- My chiropractor says I shouldn't lift any heavy objects. I think that includes grocery bags.
- I want to use everything in the kitchen so we can safely set off a bug bomb. I'll restock after those toxic fumes disappear.
- I'm boycotting all the grocery stores in the area because I think they're still trying to get away with passing off dolphin as tuna.
- The grocery store still uses plastic bags. I told them I wouldn't shop until they replace the plastic with ecologically-correct paper bags.

The Dog

- I had to make a choice. I felt taking Buster out for his daily walk was more important than going to the store and buying your lard-laden, cholesterol-packed peanut butter and chocolate chip ice cream.

Not Making Dinner

The Old Standards

- I'm too tired.
- I thought it was your turn.
- I'm not hungry.

The More Creative

- I thought it would be presumptuous of me to make something without first checking to see if you like it.

- What's your problem? We had dinner last night.
- Our relationship needs the romance of frequent restaurant meals.
- Do you smell gas? I don't think we should go near the kitchen until we speak to the gas company.
- My horoscope says I should stay away from extreme cold and extreme heat today.
- I don't have the right tools.
- Fasting is a cleansing experience; it's good for the soul.
- Cooking should be left to the professionals.

The Dog
- The dinner was right here on the table. I swear, it was all pre-pared and ready to eat. I went upstairs to get cleaned up, and the last thing I remember before jumping in the shower was letting your dog in. . . . Hey!

Not Mowing the Lawn

The Old Standards
- It's too wet.
- It's getting late and it's too dangerous to use a mower in the dark.
- I can't mow the lawn now. The sun is shining and it would burn the freshly-cut grass.

The More Creative
- Grass has feelings, too.
- I'm letting the lawn revert to its natural state.
- If the grass grows high enough, I won't need curtains.
- I'm planning on getting sheep, and they'll crop it.
- A messy lawn keeps the tax assessment down.
- I'm trying to get back to my roots.
- I reject the concept of a monoculture. Our caveman brothers never mowed their lawns.

- I'm waiting for an enterprising kid to come along. Lawns should be cut by kids. Keeps them out of trouble, and teaches them the value of a nickel.

The Dog
- The dog needs high grass so he can hide from the neighborhood cats.

Not Painting the House

The Old Standards
- The weather report said it was going to rain.
- The hardware store has to order more paint.
- My neighbor has my ladder, and he's away on vacation.

The More Creative
- This is a sensitive subject, because I'm thinking of suing the paint company. They have a ten-year guarantee on the life of their product, and look at how the finish is peeling. I just painted this place nine and a half years ago.
- Our house has landmark status. We're required to paint the place in an "original" color. We're waiting for the landmarks committee to tell us our options.
- As soon as my acrophobia clears, I'll get right to it.
- I couldn't find the right size brush.
- I couldn't find any high-altitude paint for the second story.

The Dog
- If I change the color of my house, my dog won't recognize it. She's not too bright.

Not Washing and Waxing the Car

The Old Standards
- It's supposed to rain.
- I ran out of wax.

- I'm planning on taking the kids off-road driving next weekend up by the state park. No use washing the car now, it'll only be filthy by the time we get back.

The More Creative
- Isn't there a water shortage?
- The motion I use to rub on the car wax aggravates an old war wound.
- I'm waiting until the grandkids visit. They love to go to the carwash.
- Clean cars are a hazard. They reflect light that can blind other drivers.
- The door seals leak, and every time I wash the car, water gets all over the interior.
- Shiny cars attract thieves.
- The dirt coating confuses radar detectors.
- I hear that the vacuum cleaner at my local car wash is broken. No use going if I can't clean the interior too.

The Dog
- When I try to wash the car, the dog attacks the hose; he thinks it's a snake that's trying to hurt me.

Familial

Not Having Children

The Old Standards
- We're not making enough money yet to afford kids.
- We're both too busy with our careers.
- I just don't have the patience to be a good parent.

The More Creative
- I had a traumatic childhood, and I know that being a bad parent is hereditary. I can't take the risk of having children.

- I'm focusing on my inner child—not on being a parent.
- What!? And see more of my in-laws!?
- My immune system isn't up for all those kiddy diseases.
- How can you bring a child into the world given all the horrible things that are happening?
- I did a lot of acid as a teenager and any kid I had would probably be seriously scrambled.
- It's not like we're not trying, but thank you for embarrassing us. Now everyone knows we are biologically hindered.
- We'll have the kids once we can agree on the names. But it's so hard.

The Dog
- Our dog is the baby in the family. Think of the trauma and the jealousy if we had a real baby.

Having a Lot of Children

The Old Standards
- We're Catholic.
- I came from a big family.
- There was nothing else to do.

The More Creative
- I always admired the Osmonds, the Jacksons, and the Brady Bunch.
- We can afford it.
- It's an inheritance thing. The more kids, the more money we get when my (<u>fill in name of relative</u>) dies.
- If we don't procreate, our kind will be overrun by the unworthy.
- We wanted a boy/girl, and we kept trying until we had one.
- I've always dreamed of having my own basketball team.
- This is what we get for buying a gross of cheap condoms.
- The farm needs a lot of work, and they're cheaper than paying for paid labor.

The Dog
- We saw how happy Pepper was with her litter of puppies that we decided to have a whole bunch, too.

Not Inviting the In-Laws

The Old Standards
- It would be difficult for them to make the trip.
- The kids are getting a cold and we don't want their grandparents catching it.
- It's too much of a strain on my husband/wife.

The More Creative
- Whenever the in-laws come over, the kids get overly excited and the school psychiatrist says it affects their schoolwork.
- The electric company is doing round-the-clock repair work right outside the guest room window. They'd never get any rest.
- They've already done so much for us this year, if they came here with more presents, we'd just feel too obligated.
- My mother-in-law always rearranges the furniture when she comes over. She's getting older and might get a hernia if she continues all that strenuous moving, so I don't invite her over as often.
- It's traumatic for the kids—the old man has Alzheimer's and he keeps forgetting their names.
- I don't have enough valium in the house, and my doctor's on vacation.
- I'd love to have them come, and I know they'd love to see the kids, but the boys are going camping for the weekend with their Cub Scout troop/class/other set of grandparents.

The Dog
- My father-in-law's incontinent and the dog thinks he's marking territory and responds by peeing on everything.

Not Disciplining a Child

The Old Standards
- I see my child so little, I can't stand to have any part of our precious time together dominated by discipline.
- Punishing doesn't work. I prefer to use positive reinforcement.
- Hitting a child is simply barbaric.

The More Creative
- My inner child says it's not right.
- They might bear a grudge and get me back when I'm old and feeble.
- Our culture's too oppressive already.
- I'm not setting myself up to get sued when he is old enough to have a lawyer.
- The little bugger is a masochist. So punishment for him is a reward.
- What?! And risk getting brought up on child abuse charges?
- If I wanted to punish kids, I'd move to Singapore.

The Dog
- The dog won't let me near them.

Forgetting an Anniversary

The Old Standards
- Holy mackerel! Another year gone by? I can't believe it. Time sure flies when you're having fun.
- I didn't forget. I was going to take you out next week when you least expected it.
- I didn't think you cared about anniversaries.

The More Creative
- I don't believe in this yearly stuff. I celebrate our marriage every day.

- My secretary was supposed to remind me, but she's got this jealousy problem.
- I've blocked out everything having to do with our wedding day. Any event that generated that many bills deserves to be forgotten.
- What do you mean you didn't get the card? So I guess that means you didn't get that really expensive gift I sent along with it?
- I think of anniversaries as events for old people, and I think of us as still young.
- It seems so barbaric to celebrate anniversaries. It makes it seem like you didn't really expect the marriage to last, and are happily surprised.

The Dog
- We got married on the same date that my dog died—twenty years earlier. I was ten at the time and it was very traumatic. I didn't tell you this because I wasn't aware of it myself. Just last week, my therapist helped me recover the memory I've been denying so effectively for all these years.

Entertaining

Having a Messy Home When Company Arrives

The Old Standards
- The maid was supposed to come, but she didn't.
- I had the place spotless, but the kids didn't have school today and they tore it apart.
- I meant to clean up, but I lost track of the time.

The More Creative
- I started cleaning, but I sprained my back when I lifted the couch to get the dust bunnies. I just got home from the chiro-

practor's a few minutes ago, and I'm supposed to take it easy.
- We had a break-in last night and the detectives told us not to disturb the crime scene until they take photos and dust for fingerprints.
- I know it's a mess, but I've told the kids I wouldn't clean up after them anymore, and I promised my psychotherapist I'd stick to my word.
- Don't touch a thing. This room is being used as a set for a movie. If anything is moved, we'll have a continuity problem.
- Our family therapist says that the things you leave around the house are actually suppressed messages to the other members of the family. We're waiting for him to come over and analyze this mess.

The Dog
- I had it all cleaned up, but Fergie, our Corgi, is in heat. I left the patio door open just a little bit, and seven male dogs squeezed in and started fighting over her.

Not Inviting Kids

The Old Standards
- There's nothing for children to do here.
- I'm nervous the children will hurt themselves; my place isn't babyproof.
- I'm sure you're tired of being around your kids all the time and would welcome an adult event.

The More Creative
- It's so hard for adults to find their inner children when real ones are rocketing around the place.
- My insurance agent won't allow it. The place may have some lead paint in it and I don't have window guards. Having kids here would expose me to tremendous liability.
- I used to be a teacher and whenever I'm around kids I talk in

this high-pitched, whiny voice. I sound just like a five-year-old. It's very embarrassing; I think it's also the reason my first husband left me.
- No one under five feet tall is allowed in here. I think of life as an amusement park, and of my house as a really dangerous ride.
- Kids these days are so sophisticated that they make me feel inferior.
- Having kids over here is not a good idea. There's a halfway house for sex offenders just next door.

The Dog
- Children make the dog jealous. She wants to be the only little person in the house. Okay, she bites kids.

Not Using the Fine China, Silver, and Crystal

The Old Standards
- I ran out of polish.
- The good stuff is all stored away and it would take ages to get it all out.
- I can never relax when we use that stuff. My parents would kill me if I broke any of it.

The More Creative
- We think of you as family, so we're treating you like family. It's really a compliment.
- We hid all the valuable stuff where burglars would never think to look for it, and now we can't remember where it is.
- I feel that it's essentially dishonest for us to use that stuff. We're not that rich or that formal. It makes me feel like a phony.
- I have decided never to use anything that I can't run through the dishwasher.

- We can't risk breaking that stuff. We need to keep the whole set so we can sell it to pay for Junior's college tuition.
- It turns out that a lot of that old stuff was made with lead.
- I made the mistake of not getting the good stuff out when my in-laws were here, and now, if I use it for anyone else, I get accused of disrespect.

The Dog
- Last time we used the good china, the dog licked half the gold paint off the plates.

Not Allowing Smoking

The Old Standards
- I don't mean to be intolerant, but I have these terrible allergies.
- This place is so dry that one stray spark could cause a firestorm.
- The smell of smoke gets into the curtains and the carpets and I can never get it out.

The More Creative
- No way, and push all that passive smoke into my virginal lungs? That's pulmonary rape. Your freedom stops at the tip of my nostrils. How 'bout I just spray some toxic chemicals on you?
- Smoking is old fashioned.
- Sorry, we operate under laboratory conditions here and smoke fouls all the sensors.
- Smoking reminds me of my late father who died of cancer. If I even smell smoke, I start crying and can't stop.
- Go ahead. Smoke all you want. Just don't exhale.
- No smoking here. Aliens use heat sensors and they'll detect our presence.
- The sprinkler system in here is so delicate that if you smoke, you may drown us all.

- The enemy sights on the red glow of cigarettes and shoots. Smoking attracts snipers.
- No, you can't smoke. It's a form of suicide and suicide is against my religion.

The Dog
- Old Sparky was trained to be a firedog. Whenever he smells fire, I have to crank up the fire engine and give him a ride around the block before he'll stop howling.

Serving Store-Bought Food Instead of Cooking

The Old Standards
- I didn't have time to cook.
- The stove is on the fritz.
- I had an emergency at work, and got home ten minutes ago.

The More Creative
- I wanted to cook for you, but the city has issued an alert about typhus in the water in this area.
- I know I can't compete with your marvelous cooking, so I decided to rely on professionals.
- I get so little time with you, I didn't want to waste any of it in the kitchen. With take-out food, I can concentrate on you.
- I've just learned that aluminum cookware can lead to Alzheimer's, and I haven't had a chance to replace my cookware yet.
- My hippie sister tried to use the oven as a pottery kiln and she broke it.
- Every time I cook the darn smoke alarm goes off.
- It's just too hot. I can't stand the heat, so I'm staying out of the kitchen.
- I was a cook at a summer camp, and I don't know how to cook for fewer than 500.
- If I have the dinner catered, I can write it off as entertainment.

The Dog
- I took the dog to the vet today, and the doctor prescribed a new salt-free, fat-free diet. I spent so much time cooking Foofoo's dinner that I didn't get a chance to make anything for us.

Not Inviting Someone

The Old Standards
- We've seen so much of each other lately, I'm sure she's tired of us.
- It's really not his kind of party.
- I'm pretty sure she'll be out of town at the time.

The More Creative
- We are hoping to have him over at a smaller gathering in the future.
- We thought it would be kind to wait until things were going better for him. It would be a pity if people thought he came to every party depressed.
- They see so many people through business, I naturally assumed they would want the time alone together.
- We were getting too close. People were starting to talk.
- If he came to the party, who would we talk about?

The Dog
- Dogs have this sense about people, and Buster is always barking at him. I'm taking the hint; he's not invited.

Not Serving Food

The Old Standards
- If I had to pay for food too, I couldn't afford this event.
- It's too hot to serve food.
- I thought I put "cocktails only" on the invitation.

- Given all the cases of food poisoning lately, my insurance company won't let me serve food.
- Last time I served food the bulemics hogged the bathroom for the rest of the party. Forget it.
- I want a college-style event. Just booze and dancing.
- Why have food with everyone on a diet?
- Who can serve food when it's so hard to find good help?
- I have food issues and for me to serve food just because people expect it would be severely codependent.
- We will fast in solidarity with all the hungry babies in the third world!

The Dog
- We're trying to train Newt not to beg, and the only way to do that is not to have food in the house.

Having an Undisciplined Dog

The Old Standards
- The dog is still a puppy. She'll calm down.
- He's just too cute to punish.
- I'm away all day at work and don't have the time to train the dog. I feel so guilty.

The More Creative
- The dog took our divorce badly and she's been acting up.
- We had him fixed, and he reacted by turning mean. I can't say that I blame him.
- We got the dog from the animal shelter. Her previous owners had abused her, so we have to show her we love her and earn her trust before we can discipline her.

- The dog is reacting to high-frequency sounds that humans can't hear. Some sadistic demon in the neighborhood has a dog whistle and is using it to torture my dog!
- The dog watches a lot of cartoons, and all his role models—Scooby Doo, Pluto, Odie, and Huckleberry Hound—are always getting into trouble.
- The dog's heartworm medicine makes him hyperactive.
- The lawn service put some chemicals on the lawn that are driving the dog absolutely crazy.

The Dog
- It's not my dog's fault. The other dogs in the neighborhood teach him all these bad habits.

Why the Cat Litter Box Smells

The Old Standards
- I was about to change it.
- It really smells? I guess I'm just used to it.
- I ran out of kitty litter.

The More Creative
- It's not the litter box; I live downwind of a sewage treatment plant.
- My husband/wife/child/significant other/parent bought the cheap litter.
- The odor actually serves a purpose. It lets vermin know that we have a predator in the house and it keeps them away.
- Are you aware of all the toxic chemicals they put in kitty litter? Instead of supporting those companies that make the stuff, we've decided to use plain old sand. I don't know about you, but I'd rather be subjected to a slight—but very natural—odor than contribute to the destruction of this planet.
- The cat is suffering from an intestinal problem, and that terrible odor is a side effect of the medication she's on. No matter

how much or how often we clean the box, we can't get rid of the smell.
- Socks is legally blind. If we clean out her box, she'll never find it and she'll pee all over the house.

The Dog
- It's the only way we can keep the dog from bothering Sylvester when he's trying to relieve himself.

Why the Fish Keep Dying

The Old Standards
- It's the water.
- It's the food.
- Something's wrong with the filter.

The More Creative
- I think it's my music. I love hard rock, but it appears all the fish I get are more partial to European classical or progressive jazz fusion. The people in the pet store won't let me play any of my music for the fish before I buy one. They don't want the music disturbing the other fish. I'll tell you, it's a real dilemma.
- My friends don't listen to me. I can't tell you how many times I've told them that salt water fish can't survive in a fresh water tank.
- I travel a lot and my flaky neighbor keeps forgetting to feed them.
- I think it's my roommate's fault. He/She loves to eat fish for dinner, and I believe this freaks out my fish. They get despondent, depressed, and they stop eating; eventually, they die. I tried to explain to my fish the difference between eating fish and aquarium fish, but I don't think they understood. Fish aren't the brightest of God's creatures.
- I think the tank might be the wrong size.

The Dog
- My dog keeps licking the side of the bowl for the moisture, and it scares the poor fish to death.

Why the Parrot Swears

The Old Standards
- I found out about this awful habit after I purchased him.
- The parrot has no idea what he/she is saying.
- He/She picks it up from our loud, obnoxious neighbors.

The More Creative
- He/She was raised by pirates.
- I trained him to swear so burglars would think there's some big, scary Marine living here.
- He was the class pet for a bunch of eighth graders. You know what kids are like these days.
- I think he/she watches those uncensored movies on HBO when I'm at work.
- He/She feels it's the only way to get any attention.
- I know it sounds like swearing, but if you listen closely enough you'll hear that Catherwood is really speaking Latin.
- The poor guy suffers from piles.
- My grandmother was staying with us for a couple of months and she has Tourette's Syndrome.

The Dog
- It's just noise pollution to us, but it's a survival tactic for the bird. You should see the effect it has on the dog; he won't go within ten feet of the cage when the bird starts swearing at him.

four

At Work

On the Job (The Employee)

Being Late

The Old Standards
- My alarm didn't go off.
- My car wouldn't start.
- Traffic was terrible.
- I couldn't find a parking place.
- My watch stopped.
- The weather was too wet/cold/rainy.

The More Creative
- The police were conducting a sting operation on my next door neighbor, and they used my house as their base of operations. They told me I had to stay with them until they nabbed the suspect.
- Coming in late is my contribution to the environment. It means I don't waste fuel in rush hour traffic.

- I wanted to see if you had enough initiative to start without me. Apparently, you don't.
- There was a temporary mass transit strike.
- The elevators in this building suck.
- I had a call from a customer, and that's a higher priority than getting to work on time.
- I'm practicing Mediterranean etiquette. Over there, it's fashionable to be late.
- Sorry. My chronograph was set for another time zone.
- I'm not a morning person. I thought it would be best if I came in after I had my coffee and read the paper—I'm much less cranky then.
- I'm coming in late and working late on purpose. It means that I'm here at the right time of day to serve our customers in the time zones to the west of us.
- My hair was rebelling.

The Dog
- My dog hid the car keys.

Taking a Day Off

The Old Standards
- I had to stay home and wait for a delivery.
- My kid's sick.
- I couldn't call to tell you I wouldn't be coming in, because I had to wait for the phone repairman to show up.
- I had a twenty-four-hour flu.
- My car wouldn't start.
- My (fill in relative) died and I had to go to the funeral.

The More Creative
- I had to go to the hospital. They thought I had appendicitis, but it turned out to be gas.

- So you missed me after all! I have to take a day off now and then so you'll appreciate all the things I do around here.
- I had emergency root canal surgery. My mouth was full of cotton the whole day, so I couldn't call.
- I worked until midnight yesterday, and was so tired when I left that I couldn't see straight. I don't think the car accident is really the company's fault, but I wanted to try and sleep the headache off instead of going to the doctor.
- I was preparing for my tax audit. The IRS can't believe I survive on the pittance you pay me.
- I was out of town for the weekend and they shut down the airports due to bad weather, so I couldn't get home.
- I was working from home. I can't get anything done here; it's too hectic and there are too many distractions.
- I had a horrible case of shingles and even the thought of putting on clothes nearly drove me insane.
- The jury I was on was sequestered and we weren't allowed to leave or contact the outside world.
- I was cleaning my parents' bomb shelter and I got locked in. I was there for two days before they found me. Luckily, there was plenty of food and water and a chemical toilet.
- I was at the shore when a whale beached itself. We spent the last two days trying to push the poor thing back into deep water.
- I got amnesia three days ago when I got hit in the head by a foul ball. It wasn't until this morning that I suddenly remembered who I was. Some things are still fuzzy.
- I had acute food poisoning and I couldn't leave the bathroom.
- A friend called and threatened to commit suicide. I spent eight hours on the phone trying to convince her/him life was worth living.

The Dog
- My dog, Pinkham, was hit by a car. I was so upset, the vet gave me some pills to calm me down. Unfortunately, the pills were so strong, I slept for twenty-four hours straight.

Not Getting a Raise

The Old Standards
- There's a freeze on all wages and raises.
- Raise? With the way they've been laying people off, I'm lucky I still have a job.
- My boss hates me. I think he feels threatened by me.

The More Creative
- They didn't give me a raise, but I think they're planning to offer me a piece of the company.
- I'm waiting for just the right moment to ask my boss. I'm going to do it as soon as this next project is completed.
- A raise? What is a raise, anyway? It's just money, that's all. Everybody gets a raise. I'm getting something far more valuable—more responsibility. My boss likes me so much, he has me doing his reports for him. Of course, he puts his name on the reports, but why shouldn't he? At least I get the good feeling of a job well done. In fact, I've done such a great job, my boss is getting a promotion!
- I'm glad I didn't get a raise; it would have put me into a higher tax bracket.
- I think I remind my boss of the person who had this job before me. Turns out he caught the guy sleeping with his wife.

The Dog
- We had the boss over to dinner and the damn dog kept humping his leg.

Being Fired

The Old Standards
- They got rid of my position.
- The company is relocating and I didn't want to move.
- They didn't fire me—I quit!
- My major account moved to another company.

The More Creative

- My boss was stealing my ideas and I caught him at it.
- I slept with the boss. (Or the corollary, I didn't sleep with the boss.)
- They were all threatened by my competence and my honesty, so they sabotaged me. I was stabbed in the back.
- The company brought in a consultant who recommended that all the people who really do the work be fired. Now, the company has to keep the consultant on to do the work.
- My boss wanted his daughter/son to work for the company, but he saw that she/he was insanely attracted to me.
- They plan to automate, and they fired me first because they know I'm a leader and that I'd organize the other workers.
- They rigged the toilet to do chemical urinalysis and I got caught.
- I parked in the chairman's spot.
- I was almost vested and if they didn't fire me, the fact that they had embezzled from the pension fund would have come out.
- I live for change.
- The chairman sensed that I was getting ready to quit and start a family, so he/she fired me. Boy, what a relief. I hate initiating confrontation.

The Dog

- By mistake, I ran over the boss's dog in the company parking lot.

Being Out of Work

The Old Standards

- I'm not out of work, I'm in between jobs.
- The right opportunity hasn't come along yet.
- I need some time to find myself.

The More Creative
- I wanted to spend more time with my family.
- Looking for work is a full-time job.
- I feel dirty doing such trivial work while people in (<u>fill in name of third world country</u>) are starving to death.
- I'm an artiste, not a worker!
- My therapist said that steady employment was leading me to an emotional and physical breakdown.
- I'm doing research for a book on unemployment and the benefits of food stamps.
- I'm preparing for the end of the world, which is due any day now.

The Dog
- I can't work. My dog doesn't like to be left alone for such long stretches of time.

Dating a Co-Worker

The Old Standards
- Don't be silly—we're just good friends.
- It's okay, as long as we don't report to each other.
- Where else am I going to find someone who understands the pressure we are under here?

The More Creative
- You're always talking about the company as a family; we're just making that happen.
- It's better than dating someone from a competitive company, isn't it? If I talk in my sleep, I won't be giving away any company secrets.
- Right. I finally find a way to carpool and you come up with some silly objection.

- It's really a benefit for the business. We spend a lot of off hours solving company problems.
- But you can't object. We were married in previous lives!

The Dog
- I don't care where he/she works; he's/she's the first guy/woman my dog has tolerated.

Not Completing a Report

The Old Standards
- I've been sick.
- The computer went down.
- It's in the mailroom being copied.
- My secretary quit.
- I thought it was Accounting's responsibility.

The More Creative
- It's the depleted ozone layer. I went to the beach and got burned. I couldn't move, much less walk, for five days.
- The report was done and on my desk. The only explanation I can think of is industrial espionage.
- I was putting the finishing touches on the report during that big thunderstorm last weekend when a bolt of lightning slammed into the roof. It was terrible. It fried the surge protector and burned out my computer. I lost everything.
- I came to some conclusions that I don't think should be put down on paper. We need to talk—but not here. I'll contact you.
- I realized that we can't look at this problem out of context. The report needs to be expanded, but that will take time.

The Dog
- The final report was on a disk I was going to bring into work and print out, but my puppy got into my briefcase and chewed up *everything*.

Not Making Coffee

The Old Standards
- I don't know how.
- I didn't take the last cup.
- I was in a hurry.
- It's not in my job description.

The More Creative
- You're insulting my gender to suggest that I should be the one to make the coffee.
- I don't care what you say, if I'm going to make the coffee, I'm going to run detergent through the machine to clean it. I won't be responsible for someone catching some awful disease from that filthy machine.
- I refuse to make coffee until good, strong brewed tea is also made available.
- Caffeine is a drug. I will be a user, but don't ask me to be a pusher.
- It's not my turn. My turn comes right after the CEO's.

The Dog
- I'd love to, but I have this odd skin infection on my hands that I caught from Stinky. . . .

Business (The Employer)

Raising Prices

The Old Standards
- Our costs are rising, too. It's inflation.
- Give us a break. We haven't raised our prices in years.
- Our stockholders are demanding bigger dividends.

The More Creative
- Our major suppliers in (<u>fill in name of a troubled country</u>) are experiencing some government problems.
- We've got to build up some funds to cover insurance costs. . . . you know—it's that medical reform stuff.
- We're expecting a government price freeze, and we'd rather have our prices frozen at a level that leaves us some working room.
- Our new strategy is to give rebates, but in order to do that, we have to raise prices.
- We did it for you. Now you can claim you use only the most expensive ingredients.

The Dog
- We have to cover a big tax liability. The company dog bit the auditor and he nailed us.

Not Giving a Raise

The Old Standards
- There's no money in the budget.
- We can't give you a raise now, but we'll give you a bonus later.
- We'd like to give you a raise, but you're already at the top salary for your job.
- We can't; last quarter's numbers were terrible.

The More Creative
- I can't give you a raise. Everyone knows I really like you. If I gave you a raise, they'd assume we were sleeping together.
- I meant to give you a raise, but I got behind on my paperwork that week you were out sick, and I missed the deadline to put in for one for you.

- You wanted a raise? Why didn't you tell me? You seemed so happy.
- I wouldn't be doing you a favor if I gave you a raise. It would make you so highly-paid that it would be hard for you to find another job (which you may need to do, given the shape that this place is in).
- A raise? The boss hasn't had a raise—or a vacation—in five years. Who do you think you are??
- You don't want a raise. Most of it would just go to taxes.
- Two big consultants came in to teach us ways to raise our corporate morale. They got paid the money that had been set aside for raises.

The Dog
- The boss bought an incredibly expensive show dog which has to eat only expensive, top-quality beef. That dog ate the money for your raise.

Not Repairing Something

The Old Standards
- We don't have the right parts in stock; we'll have to special-order them.
- We don't have the right tools.
- We only repair stuff we sold.

The More Creative
- We've lost the Swede who can translate the manual.
- It's a union job—if I fixed it, they'd shut down this whole complex.
- I could fix it, but it wouldn't be fair to you. . . . It's a much better value for you to get a new one.
- We couldn't reach you to get your approval to go ahead and

order the (<u>fill in name of an obscure piece of hardware</u>) that was needed.
- The boss was out, so there was no one around to approve the project.
- I waited because there's a rumor of a recall. If that's the case, you'll get it repaired for free.

The Dog
- The dog buried the part we needed.

Shipping Late

The Old Standards
- I didn't know there was a rush.
- The shipment got held up in customs.
- We shipped it on-time, but someone had given us the wrong address. When we found out, we turned it around right away.

The More Creative
- That was a real order? We thought your financial guys just wanted to enter the invoice against this year instead of accruing the funds.
- That product's nowhere near ready to ship. The saleswoman should have told you that, but I guess she just wanted to get her numbers up to make her bonus for that quarter. Don't worry; we'll fire her.
- Your paperwork must have been part of the mail that was burned in that post office fire.
- It was shipped, but no one at your place would sign for it, so it came back to us.
- The bankruptcy judge told us not to ship anything.
- Our company team made it into the softball league finals, and the whole shipping department was at an "away" game.

- The damn ecologists made us wait to see if any more of those Asian vipers had gotten into the boxes. They said it was unlikely that there would have been only three.

The Dog
- Dog hairs got into the air filters and shut down the air conditioning that cools the computers and they crashed. We've been trying to figure out what's gone out and what hasn't. Thank goodness you called.

Firing Someone

The Old Standards
- There's nothing wrong with you. The company is just taking another direction.
- You're getting old, and this is a young person's business. The clients expect fresh blood.
- We're replacing you with a machine.
- I just don't think you're right for this place.

The More Creative
- The company is being taken over by the CIA, and you failed security clearance. Of course this is top secret, and we'll deny it in public.
- We have information which indicates that our competitors are reading your mind telepathically. We can't keep you here where you can see our trade secrets.
- You're a great worker, but we've decided to concentrate on our softball team.
- Don't blame me. Blame the Asians; they're taking all the jobs.
- We're going high-tech and we need people who grew up using computers.
- If it were up to me, I'd keep you, but the management consultants developed a sophisticated formula which balances

productivity and seniority. According to their calculations, you're the one who gets fired.

The Dog
- If the boss were in a better mood, maybe I could fight for you. But his beloved dog, Hoover, just died . . .

five

Matters of the Mind

Not Recycling

The Old Standards
- Keeping used bottles and cans around just attracts vermin and germs.
- It's too complicated. Some plastics are recyclable while others aren't; I can't keep it straight.
- I can't get to the dump—it's only open while I'm at work.
- I can't find those official recycling bags in the store.

The More Creative
- Recycling is a conspiracy against American industry. What's wrong with making more new steel?
- The recycling plants create more hazardous waste.
- I don't recycle because I precycle; it's much safer environmentally.
- I'm too tired; I've already biked fifteen miles today.

- We have a homeless person in the neighborhood who picks the cans out of the garbage for us.
- I hate the idea of recycling things. I don't want things that other people have used before. I only want new things.
- Our kitchen's too small as it is. We certainly don't have room for all those recycling bins.

The Dog
- With all the dogs in the neighborhood, I'm afraid one will get his or her head stuck in all that twine we're supposed to tie up our discarded newspapers with and choke to death.

Wearing Fur

The Old Standards
- It's *so* warm.
- If I don't, someone else will.
- I didn't really buy it, it was my grandmother's.

The More Creative
- I have a rare skin disease. If I get within five feet of synthetic fibers, I break out in a splotchy, ugly, red rash.
- We're all animals anyway.
- My husband is very self-conscious of his hairy back, and I want him to feel comfortable.
- There was a bumper crop of mink this year and if they weren't made into coats, they'd have died slowly and painfully from disease.
- Because I can.
- Fur is more politically correct than synthetics. Animals are, after all, a renewable resource.
- Wearing fur is my way of protesting hunting. The hunters learn they can't shoot at every furry thing they see.

- The Bible says that animals were put on earth to serve man's needs.

The Dog
- My dog wears fur, why shouldn't I?

Hunting

The Old Standards
- If I don't, someone else will.
- I eat what I kill. Nothing goes to waste.
- If it was okay for our ancestors, it's okay for me.

The More Creative
- I was in the special forces where I was trained to kill. It's very difficult to unlearn all that training. If I couldn't hunt animals, I might start going after humans.
- If we don't hunt (<u>fill in favorite animal</u>), they'll overpopulate the region and destroy the crops.
- I'm just protecting my livestock from predators. (NOTE: Tough excuse for urban settings.)
- If I didn't hunt, the guys at work would think I'm a sissy.
- If we humans didn't continue to show strength, the animals would band together, rise up, and take over.
- I'm just practicing for Armageddon.
- Hunting is my way of staying in touch with my primordial side. Ultimately it makes me more sensitive and understanding of my ecosystem.
- Thank goodness it's me. At least I respect the animals I hunt.

The Dog
- If I didn't hunt, Old Blue would probably die of boredom. Hunting dogs have to hunt.

Parking in a Handicap Space

The Old Standards
- It was the only space available.
- I'll only be a second.
- Define handicap.

The More Creative
- I hurt my foot the other day, and I'm still limping.
- I thought they were setting aside a space for bad golfers.
- My wife/husband/child/friend sitting over there in the car is saying some pretty stupid things today. Doesn't that count?
- The space was open and it seemed unecological to drive all the way to another spot.
- I have to be near the store's door. If my spouse/ child / friend/relative can't see me, he/she gets an anxiety attack.
- Handicap parking? I thought some graffiti artist was responsible for plastering those silly images all over the city's parking lots.
- If they want to be treated like everyone else, why should they have better parking?

The Dog
- I'm afraid my dog might get dognapped. The handicap parking space is conveniently located right across from where I shop and I can keep an eye on him.

Being a Bigot

The Old Standards
- I just can't relate.
- My daddy and granddaddy can't be wrong.
- Some of my best friends are (<u>fill in minority</u>).

- Standardized tests show that (<u>fill in name of group</u>) are less intelligent.
- Since they're so much better at sports/entertaining/money matters than we are, it's only right to limit them in other areas.
- Each group should take care of its own—that's the way the world works.
- They have their traditions and I have mine. Hating them is one of my traditions.
- If we were meant to like people who were different from us, we'd all be the same.
- If I hung out with them, my friends would shun me.
- It's a gene-pool thing, and somebody peed in theirs.

The Dog
- It's not my fault, my dog, Wallace, just can't stand (<u>fill in minority</u>).

Eating Red Meat

The Old Standards
- I'm a carnivore, damn it.
- It's the American way.
- It's the best source of protein.

The More Creative
- People from the beef lobby threatened to do something to my family if I didn't eat more red meat. I think they're running scared.
- I personally hate eating red meat, but I have to do it so I can produce enough blood for my sister's transfusions.
- If we didn't eat beef, we'll be overrun with cows. Hell, the country will look just like India in a couple of years.

- The soy beans keep falling through the grill of my barbecue.
- My friend the local butcher has six kids, a wife who's paraplegic, and a second mortgage on his house. They need my business.
- If I don't eat red meat at the sales meeting, the guys will think I'm a pushover.
- I eat red meat to keep my teeth healthy. Our incisors were designed to tear flesh.
- Eating red meat fulfills my killer instinct and makes me a more effective negotiator.

The Dog
- It's the only thing my dog will eat.

Joining a Club That Discriminates

The Old Standards
- It's close to my house.
- I didn't know it was so exclusive until after I become a member.
- It was my grandfather's membership and it's a family tradition.

The More Creative
- I'm doing an exposé. Please don't blow my cover.
- What are you talking about? The groundskeeper is black and I'm certain there're some Hispanics working in the kitchen.
- Do you know how much it would cost to put in a female locker room?
- If enough of us open-minded people join, we'll be able to change the place. If none of us belong, it will never change.
- The club simply represents the neighborhood, which happens to be segregated.
- I'm just exercising my constitutional right to free association.
- I wouldn't belong, but it's where I do all of my business.

The Dog
- It's the only place in the area that offers kennel services for pedigreed dogs. Lord Mountjoy can't stay just anywhere when we go to Europe.

Intellectual/Cultural

Not Reading the Daily Newspaper

The Old Standards
- I just don't have the time.
- I listen to the news on my car radio while I commute.
- I get my news from TV.

The More Creative
- Newspapers are too slow; I tap straight into the news services via my computer.
- I'm in recovery, and I have to focus on saving myself, not the whole world.
- The newspaper ink always comes off on my hands and clothes.
- The only paper worth reading is *The New York Times*. But I refuse to read a paper that's so snotty that it doesn't include comics.
- My father always hid behind the paper, and I swore I would never put the newspaper between my family and me.
- The only time I have to read the paper is on the train. But I have never been able to master the executive origami art of folding a paper down to a column.

The Dog
- I hope to get back to reading the paper soon. But, for the moment, the puppy has claimed the paper for other purposes.

Not Going to a Museum

The Old Standards
- It's too boring.
- I don't have the time.
- It'll be too crowded.

The More Creative
- I could make half the things I see in museums—especially that crappy modern cubist impressionistic stuff.
- Video is my medium of choice. All others are so primitive.
- It's a beautiful day, why waste it in a musty old museum?
- It's awful outside, why risk catching a cold trying to get to some musty old museum?
- I hate museums. It's all about dead artists, and it makes me feel like such a voyeur of morbidity.

The Dog
- Weekend days are the only chance I can spend some quality time with my dog, Pollack. Unfortunately, dogs aren't allowed in museums.

Not Going to the Opera/Ballet/Symphony

The Old Standards
- I'm no namsy-pamsy.
- The tickets are too expensive.
- I don't own a tuxedo.

The More Creative
- My opera glasses are in the shop.
- I refuse to watch a performance that's in a language other than English.

- Any more than three musicians is just too confusing.
- I don't need to go to the opera. I saw the fat lady sing at the end of the Yankee game last night.
- My ex-wife/-husband used to sneak around on her/his tiptoes all the time; it ruined ballet for me.
- I already had a nap today.

The Dog
- My dog ate the libretto.

Not Reading the Classics

The Old Standards
- I read most of them in high school.
- Why live in the past?
- The print's too small, and the books have too many pages. Who has time to read a 500-page book?

The More Creative
- My library only stocks new titles.
- I can't understand half the things the characters in some of those books are saying. We don't use those big words nowadays; it's pretentious.
- Authors like Clancy, Grisham, and Steel write about real problems that face real people. I don't ever remember Dickens ever writing about sexy lawyers in submarines, do you?
- Most of the classics are so sexist. Even the women wrote under men's names. What were they thinking?
- They've made movies out of most of the classics, and I've seen them all.

The Dog
- I named my dog Shakespeare. Isn't that enough?

Not Owning a Computer

The Old Standards
- It's too expensive.
- My old typewriter is just fine.
- I'm too intimidated by the technology.
- I use the one at work.

The More Creative
- I'm waiting for the prices to go down.
- I'm waiting until Apple and IBM become completely compatible.
- I'm afraid I'll get too lazy and forget to back up all my documents. A friend's machine crashed before he/she saved all of his/her work and he's/she's in a mental institution now.
- I read somewhere that extended use of computers can cause a crippling disease of the hands called carpal tunnel syndrome, and can also damage one's eyesight from staring at the screen for too long.
- The wiring in my house is unreliable, and the last thing I need is a power failure while I'm in the middle of writing a report or something.

The Dog
- The tapping of the keys, although relatively inaudible to me, drives my dog crazy.

Have any creative excuses for getting through life's daily grind? They can be real or imagined, used by you or used on you. The more the merrier. If so, send them to:

EXCUSES
c/o St. Martin's Press
175 Fifth Avenue
New York, N.Y. 10010

We're sorry, but no compensation or credit can be given. Hey, it's not our rule, it's our publisher's.